THE WEST
AT WAR 1939–45

THE WEST AT WAR 1939–45

NICK MADDOCKS

SUTTON PUBLISHING
ITV WEST AND TESTIMONY FILMS

First published in the United Kingdom in 2005 by
Sutton Publishing Limited · Phoenix Mill
Thrupp · Stroud · Gloucestershire · GL5 2BU
in association with ITV West

This book is based upon the ITV West television series produced
by Testimony Films.

British Library Cataloguing in Publication Data
A catalogue record for this book is available from the British Library.

ISBN 0-7509-4110-3

Dedicated to my nephew Stanley, in the hope that this book
is the closest he ever comes to war.

Typeset in Garamond 3 11.5/15pt.
Typesetting and origination by
Sutton Publishing Limited.
Printed and bound in England by
J.H. Haynes & Co. Ltd, Sparkford.

Contents

Julian Fane

Bill Lacey

Joe Trinder

Frank Henn

Bill Stanton

Len Llewellyn

Bill Green

Keith Aldridge

Mary Lalonde

Maurice Ryan

John Salinas

David Wood

Ken Davenport

Geoff Young

Derek Horsford

Dennis Greenslade

Ted Davis

Acknowledgements

I would like to thank all the people who have helped with the writing of this book, and the making of the ITV West television series which it accompanies, in particular James Garrett from ITV West for his continuing support and belief in local programming. Thanks also to Ifty Khan, Lesley Ellett and Molly Watkin from ITV West for help and advice along the way.

Special thanks go to all at Testimony Films, especially to Steve Humphries for giving me the opportunity to produce such an important series, and to Clair Titley for her tireless commitment and enthusiasm. Thanks also to Daniel De Waal for his invaluable advice, to cameraman Michael Pharey for his skill and patience, to Mary Parsons and Lizi Cosslett for making Testimony Films such a great place to work and to Mike Humphries. Thank you also to Sally Humphries for the use of Rose Cottage, and to Bridget Blythe and all at Pink House Post Productions in Bristol.

I would of course like to thank all the veterans' associations, societies, museums and individuals who helped us along the way. There are too many to list individually, but special thanks go to Major Claud Rebbeck and George Streatfield at the Soldiers of Gloucestershire Museum, to John Hamblett, to Bill Edwardes, Chairman of the 43rd Wessex Division Association, to David Watkins and Wing Commander Kenneth MacKenzie from 501 Squadron, and to Iain Arnold from the Hurricane Association. Thanks also to Norman Date of the Bristol branch of the Merchant Navy Association and to the many others from the local branches of the Merchant Navy, Royal Navy, Normandy Veterans and Burma Star Associations who very kindly put us in touch with their members. Many apologies to anyone I may have omitted.

Of course this book would have been impossible without the contributions of the veterans who gave up their time to share their stories with us, and many thanks go to those we filmed: Kenneth Lee, Joe Trinder, Frank Henn, Julian Fane, Bill Lacey, Len Llewellyn, Dennis Smith, Bill Green, Keith Aldridge, Jim Loftus, Mary Lalonde, Bill Stanton, Geoff and Margrit Young, Maurice Ryan,

Dennis Greenslade, Leslie Blake, Bess Cummings, John Salinas, Jim Pratt, Ted Davis, Ken Davenport, Derek Horsford, Tom Packwood, David Wood, Doug Allen and Cyril Stephens. Unless otherwise stated, all photographs are the copyright of the interviewees/Testimony Films.

Thanks, of course, to all at Sutton Publishing for their belief in this book.

Finally a very special thank you to my family, Jill, Ivor and Kate Maddocks, and to Nemia Brooks, for encouragement and support along the way.

Introduction

The year 2005 marks the sixtieth anniversary of the end of the Second World War. During the five and a half years of bitter fighting that raged between 1939 and 1945, some 500,000 British and Commonwealth servicemen gave their lives while on active service, and many more were wounded or maimed. It is almost impossible to put a figure on the number of soldiers, sailors and airmen from the West of England who fought during the conflict, but in 2005 many thousands will gather in the cities, towns and villages of our region to pay their respects to friends and colleagues who made the ultimate sacrifice in the pursuit of freedom. This book, and the ITV West television series which it accompanies, were commissioned to commemorate this important anniversary, and to pay tribute to the courage, dignity and humour of the men and women from our region whose lives were forever touched by the events that began in Europe in the autumn of 1939.

Many books have focused on life on the home front during the Second World War, but a local study of front-line experience has been a comparatively neglected area. For over a year the production team at Testimony Films in Bristol collected first-hand accounts from many hundreds of veterans, and were provided with graphic and moving descriptions of action seen in all the major campaigns. We are most grateful to the countless local and national organisations, clubs and societies that helped to put us in touch with their members. It is sad to note that as the years take their toll, many of these organisations will close down following the sixtieth anniversary commemorations. Many of the veterans we contacted, however, were not part of any official organisation, preferring instead to put the past behind them in an attempt to forget the horrors of war. Some of them were, quite understandably, reluctant or even unwilling to share their memories with us, while others told their story for perhaps the first time. Quite often, these were among the most powerful testimonies we heard, and we were frequently humbled by the frank and often harrowing accounts we recorded.

Research began at the beginning of 2004, expertly guided by Series Producer Steve Humphries and since then researcher Clair Titley and I have personally met and spoken to local veterans with vastly differing wartime experiences – from those who escaped Dunkirk, flew in the Battle of Britain or sailed in the Battle of the Atlantic, to those who landed on the beaches of Normandy on D-Day or emerged victorious from the jungles of Burma. We have heard the most remarkable stories from submariners, airborne troops and spies; from tank commanders, French resistance operatives and prisoners of war. Indeed, from the outset we realised that our most difficult problem would be in deciding which stories we should include and which we would have to leave out.

Of course, it was impossible for us to provide a detailed history of the Second World War in just six short programmes and as a result several significant theatres of war have unfortunately been omitted, among them the vitally important victories in North Africa and Italy. However, we have been able to tell for the first time the little known roles played by some our region's most illustrious fighting forces, the Gloucestershire Regiment's heroic defence outside Dunkirk in 1940, and 501 (County of Gloucester) Hurricane Squadron's success in the Battle of Britain among them. In fact, such was the importance and heroic nature of the Glosters' actions during the Battle of France, we decided to dedicate two programmes, and two chapters of this book, to their incredible sacrifice. Given the current uncertainty with regard to the regiment's future, we are honoured to pay proper respect to their past glories.

One important consideration we had to look at early on in our research was the obvious question of what do we mean by the West? The ITV West region itself has clear boundaries and reaches roughly from Gloucestershire in the north to Somerset in the south, and from Wiltshire in the east to Bristol in the west. However, we had to decide whether we should include just those people born and raised in our region or add those born elsewhere but living here now, or perhaps those who served with local units. Ultimately, we decided that as long as a potential interviewee fulfilled one of these three criteria, they would be eligible for consideration. In fact, this definition proved invaluable when researching the roles of the Royal and Merchant Navy, for although the West Country has a long and well-known maritime history, a large majority of the sailors we spoke to were born outside our region. Of course, the very nature of a life at sea means that sailors will often move around from port to port and frequently settle outside the area of their birth. As a result, Chapter Four includes the experiences of merchant seamen from London and Liverpool, who now live in the West Country, as well as testimony from a Royal Navy volunteer from Gloucestershire.

The chapters in the book are arranged chronologically, beginning with the Battle of France and ending with the conclusion of the war in the Far East. Each chapter begins with a brief introduction to provide a general overview to the personal testimony that follows, and the memories of the veterans are illustrated with many personal photographs and documents, which help bring their stories to life. We are very grateful to those we interviewed for trusting us with their precious memorabilia, and for allowing us to reproduce it here. It was very moving to see how many veterans kept photographs of friends they had lost in battle, and once again we are honoured to be able to include these also.

Due to time constraints, and for reasons beyond our control, not all the veterans we filmed were included in the television series. It is difficult to tell a complicated story in a 30-minute television slot and often the programmes had to be edited for the sake of simplicity. Thankfully, however, writing this book has enabled us to include some of the stories that had to be left out of the series, particularly in the case of the D-Day chapter, which we have extended to include the beach landings and the incredible story of the 43rd Wessex Division. In fact not long after research began, we had intended to dedicate one of the programmes to the Wessex Division, who fought continuously from June 1944 to the end of the war in Europe. However, so long and varied was their action that it became hard to know quite where to start! We hope that the inclusion of Geoff Young's remarkable story in Chapter Five goes some way to redressing this.

Finally, I would like to pay special tribute to one particular veteran. Joe Trinder was born in the small village of Bibury in Gloucestershire and grew up in one of the picturesque terraced cottages in Arlington Row. When war broke out, Joe, along with many young men from Bibury, joined the territorials of the 5th Battalion of the Glosters. In 1940, he sailed to France with the British Expeditionary Force and his adventures fighting the Germans in the withdrawal to Dunkirk are movingly told in the first two chapters. After Dunkirk, Joe went back to France with the 43rd Wessex Division, before finally returning home to his wife in Bibury. Joe was one of the first veterans we filmed. His descriptions of everyday life in France were among the most eloquent we heard and it was a pleasure to listen as he recounted his experiences with passion and humour. Joe died in 2004 at the age of 93. We were all very sad to learn of his passing, but glad that we had had the opportunity to meet such a wonderful old gentleman and record his stories for future generations.

As the years pass by, fewer and fewer veterans will make their annual journey to cenotaphs around the region, and within decades the horrors of life on the front line during the Second World War will be beyond living memory. Perhaps through the testimony which follows, their stories will live on for years to come.

Nick Maddocks
January 2005

Joe Trinder, 1911–2004.

ONE

LAST MAN, LAST ROUND

The Glosters and the Battle of France

When war broke out on 3 September 1939 two battalions of the Gloucestershire Regiment were selected to go to France with the British Expeditionary Force (BEF). The 2nd Battalion, based at Seaton Barracks in Plymouth, was made up of regular soldiers like Jim Loftus and Bill Lacey and because they were already trained for battle, they set sail for France in early October. Officers like Julian Fane whose training at the Royal Military Academy, Sandhurst, had been cut short by the outbreak of war joined the battalion in France. The 5th Battalion was formed from a combination of Territorial soldiers and recently conscripted 'Belisha Boys', the first militia men called up by Secretary of State Leslie Hore-Belisha. New recruits like Joe Trinder and Len Llewellyn served alongside trained soldiers including Bill Stanton and young officer Frank Henn, who were drafted in to bolster the strength of the battalion. Having undertaken a period of further training in England, the 5th Battalion sailed for France in January 1940.

The first few months in France marked the period known as the Phoney War. The Glosters passed the time training and digging trenches in the frozen fields, wondering if and when they would see action. The harsh conditions they faced were evocatively captured by a newsreel photographer when he filmed the 5th Battalion on exercise in the village of Thumeries at the end of January 1940. Both battalions were then posted in front of the Maginot Line, the supposedly impenetrable fortified defences built by the French to keep the Germans out, and it was here that many men had their first encounters with the German Army. One particularly fierce exchange occurred on 3 March in the town of Grindorff, where Sergeant Bill Adlam became the first TA soldier of the war to receive the Military Medal after he recovered a Bren gun while under fire.

The 5th Glosters training in the snow during the Phoney War. *(IWM F2333)*

On 10 May 1940 the Phoney War was brought to a swift conclusion as German forces began their lightning assault on the Low Countries: German Panzers and paratroopers began to sweep across Western Europe. In response the British Army was sent into Belgium, which had previously been out of bounds because of its neutrality, and on 14 May the Glosters made their way up to the plains of Waterloo, where they hoped to settle in for battle. Initially this

The Glosters at the Battle of Quatre Bras during the Waterloo campaign, 1815. *(National Gallery of Victoria, Melbourne, Australia/The Bridgeman Art Library)*

choice of location brought some comfort to the men because the Glosters had acquitted themselves admirably against French forces on that famous battlefield during the Napoleonic Wars. But within hours, news arrived that the Germans had broken through the French ranks and the Glosters were forced to withdraw. It was a frustrating time for both battalions because the men were keen to stand and hold the line, but such was the speed of the German advance that they were in danger of being cut off. Six days and nights were spent in a constant cycle of withdrawing, stopping, digging in, then withdrawing again and at one point the 5th Battalion marched an incredible 95 miles in just 83 hours, a feat all the more admirable considering there was little in the way of food or rest. The difficulties were exacerbated by the constant threat of aerial bombardment from the dreaded Stuka dive-bombers and the fact that many roads were clogged with refugees. In the circumstances, it was perhaps not surprising that men like Len Llewellyn were separated from the rest of their battalion and forced to make their own way to the coast.

On 19 May the 5th Glosters were eventually able to hold a defensive position on the banks of the River Escault and it was here that gunner Bill Stanton was particularly successful in preventing the Germans from crossing in rubber boats. Just 4 miles away the 2nd Battalion was passing

through the town of Tournai in a truck convoy when it became bogged down in heavy traffic. For the Luftwaffe it was too good an opportunity to miss, and Julian Fane, Jim Loftus and Bill Lacey all have vivid memories of the ensuing aerial bombardment which cost the lives of 194 men of the battalion. By 22 May German Panzer divisions had reached the outskirts of Boulogne and the decision was made to evacuate the BEF from Dunkirk. But if this plan was to be successful, selected divisions of the British Army would have to defend a perimeter around the French port to allow the exhausted troops time to escape. The Glosters were among those chosen for the role.

On 23 May, the 5th Battalion was instructed to hold the small villages of Arneke and Ledringhem, which lie some 10 miles south of Dunkirk. The following day, the depleted 2nd Battalion was ordered to take up positions in the strategically important hillside town of Cassel, which lies on the main road to Dunkirk and commands spectacular views all the way to the coast. Indeed Cassel had been used as a headquarters by Marshal Foch who commanded Allied forces during the First World War and was also the hill upon which the Grand Old Duke of York, of nursery rhyme fame, famously marched his 10,000 men in 1793.

In the days that followed, both Glosters battalions were subjected to fierce German attack from tanks, artillery, infantry and, of course, from the air, but their defence was nothing less than resolute. Their orders had been to hold the line at all costs and if that meant to the last man, last round, then so be it.

JULIAN FANE

I'd intended to go into the Army, so I went to Sandhurst and we were there when war was declared. They immediately cut short our course and so we completed only six months. But still, we were excited by the thought of war and quite frankly we couldn't wait to join our regiments. We couldn't think otherwise, that's what we wanted to do. I went to the Glosters, the regiment of my selection, a very fine regiment who had a very interesting and excellent history and who actually had been commanded by my uncle. My father commanded the 12th Lancers, so it was a question of one or the other. I arrived in France near Lille, where I joined the 2nd Battalion at the age of 19 and was posted to B Company. The thing that impressed me about the 2nd Battalion

Julian Fane's training at Sandhurst was cut short when war broke out in 1939.

was that there were a lot of long-service non-commissioned officers and sergeants, which was an enormous help to a 19-year-old 2nd lieutenant, and they more or less took charge of us, rather than us taking charge of them, in the initial stages of the war. I was always grateful for that. The immediate reaction that I had when I arrived in France was they were busy teaching us to dig trenches and build barbed-wire fences, which I rather thought was not the kind of training I had expected for a modern war. It seemed to be to be based on the old 1914–18 war. I also noticed that a lot of the tactical side seemed not to consider the possibility of a mechanised attack. We were still marching on our feet and using not very up-to-date weapons.

We started moving on 14 May and made our way slowly in transport or on Shanks's pony to end up on the plains of Waterloo. I thought to myself, 'Well, this is a good start for a battle.' Then we deployed and we waited. After that we were overwhelmed because the flanks were never secured, in my opinion. The French had trained to fight in the Maginot Line and I don't think they were as prepared as we might be to fight in the open. People fell back on both sides of us and we really had what I would like to call a fighting withdrawal. Some people had the temerity to call it a retreat, but a retreat indicates a sort of disorderly arrangement, whereas our withdrawal was very closely co-ordinated. We were standing to fight all the time and preparing to hold a line. And it infuriated us because we were lacking in sleep and we were moving an awful lot. You'd dig a hole, a defensive line, and sometimes you'd get a bullet or two whistle in your direction, but there was no attack in front of you. You were then told to fall back to another line and you didn't know what the hell was happening. All the troops were getting browned off. They didn't want to keep going back. They wanted to get settled and have a fight. All the Glosters, including myself, felt very despondent and disappointed that we should be withdrawing so often. It's not what we'd joined the Army to do.

On 19 May we were in a convoy of trucks leading out of Belgium when we came to the town of Tournai. The roads were clogged with refugees and cars and carts with mattresses on top, all fleeing down the same road that we were motoring down. The Germans then started bombing the convoy and about three trucks behind me they hit our ammunition truck. Things were exploding in every direction. My platoon was walking section by section down the road and I jumped into a ditch. The aeroplanes then started strafing the road, the refugees, everybody in sight. You could hear the bullets whistling over your head, and of course they killed innumerable people – women, children, babies, as well as soldiers. There's nothing you can do except keep your head down and hope.

Digging trenches in the frozen fields of Northern France. *(IWM O426)*

French troops and refugees hide from aerial attack. *(IWM F4480)*

That's all you could do. Once it had finished you had to get up and survey the scene and rally the troops and get moving. There was no emotion other than fear. There was nothing else you could do.

We continued on for several days and arrived eventually at a place called Cassel. On entering the town we found that it had been very severely bombed, that there were many French corpses and lots of animals had been killed, lots of the horses used for towing guns. And so we had a horrible and unpleasant job of clearing all the mess up before we could deploy. Unfortunately, a lot of the people were still living in their houses and had to be kicked out, which was unsatisfactory, but there it was. We couldn't hold the town without using the houses.

We actually had the order that we were to stay behind to cover Dunkirk and I thought to myself, 'Last man, last round.' I'd heard that before in my military history and I thought, 'My goodness, I didn't think this would happen to me so soon in my military career.' But we didn't have time to be worried. We got busy developing our defences and then of course we were attacked repeatedly by tanks, artillery and aircraft, so we had a very busy time and suffered quite a few casualties. Obviously we realised that our chances were negligible and that the Germans had completely outflanked us.

Our platoon was on the left, guarding an approach to Cassel on a sort of winding road, and at one stage a German despatch rider was sent up. As he arrived towards our position he was shot. We dragged him in to interrogate him and he had a piece of paper on him which purported to come from their artillery battery to say that they were withdrawing, which was obviously a trick. He had been shot in the head and was dying, so we took his helmet off. All his head had been blown apart and his brains fell out of his helmet.

Not far from me was a young officer and he was put into a position covering a rather open piece of ground. He was in a house which had been prepared for defence and he held out with his platoon for quite a long time, but eventually most of them were killed because they were shelled and attacked. So battles were going on one side of me and behind me in woodland. Obviously when the Germans started breaking into our own company positions and had to be repulsed we had no reserves to deploy, so we just had to hold where we could.

I was invited by the company commander to go and take out a tank, which was in the adjoining company's backyard. So I got the man who held the PIAT anti-tank rifle and we made our way up through the trees in a sort of woodland area. We got very close, about 50 yards from the tank. He got his aim just right and I was lying next door to him. Suddenly, just as he was about to fire, a whole lot of mortar bombs landed just in front of us. He was wounded and I got him to the stretcher-bearers who were behind us. I dragged him a bit of the way and I put a field dressing on him. But I had to leave him. I think his liver was exposed and I don't know whether he lived at all. The stretcher-bearers were very brave.

I'm not a poker player. I'm very bad at assessing risks and the odds, but obviously the chances of getting killed were quite great and we were all aware of the fact that, in the Glosters, our chances were diminishing very rapidly.

BILL LACEY

I was brought up by my grandparents in Ilfracombe and when my grandfather died I moved up to Bristol to join the rest of my family. I must have heard something about the Army, so I went along to the Colston Hall in Bristol to join up. In the April (1939) I was 18 and I joined up in August. I was very proud to be a Gloster.

Bill Lacey had his first encounter with the Germans near Waterloo.

We went over to France and then up in front of Waterloo. One night, I was standing up in front of where we were digging in and I heard somebody coming along. I thought it was one of our officers, checking up as to whether I was on guard, so I got my bayonet between my legs ready to challenge him, but when I looked up there was a German hat and God knows what. Automatically I just brought up the bayonet and there was a grunt and that was it. I think it must have gone right through his heart. It went straight through his chest anyhow. He was dead right away; that was it. And the awful part about it was, his weight on the bayonet pulled me over and I could have fallen on top of him.

Then I went down to where they was digging the trenches and I was babbling, trying to explain what had happened. I was incoherent. They carted him away and I was left there still on guard. I was cleaning the bayonet out – putting it in the ground and cleaning it out that way. Ever after, I always thought that the whole German Army was after me for it. I never expected to do that sort of thing. We'd only just moved up into position and this happened within two or three hours. It just didn't seem real. It really upset me, but I wasn't given time to think about it because the platoon left straight away and we did an 11-mile march before we stopped again and took up positions.

We was retreating all the while but funnily enough we didn't feel defeated: that was the whole point. Every time we stopped and took up positions we found that the French had given way on our flank and the Germans was moving around on our rear, so we had to move back. But we were ready for them at any time, all the way. All the time this went on, right through Belgium, right back to Cassel. You had a lot of prams and carts in the road where the civilians were moving out. Then planes would come over and strafe us, but they didn't care if there were refugees. They'd just machine gun the whole lot. We was getting no

The roads in France and Belgium were often crowded with refugees. *(IWM F4424)*

sleep and we was absolutely exhausted by the time we got to Tournai. We was sleeping on the march, walking automatically, and the next minute you would bump into the person in front because you didn't realise they'd stopped. You just lost track of time and feeling. If it was a rest break, you'd be down on the ground right away, taking as much rest as you could. But once it came to getting up again, it was quite a struggle. You were bullied into getting up.

At Tournai there was quite a wide road. There we were on the trucks, just enjoying the first ride of the lot after marching all the way through Belgium and we had only gone a mile or so when the planes started coming over. Somebody said, 'They're ours,' and the next minute we heard the bombs being dropped. Everybody bailed out of the trucks with their rifles. I got out, but I didn't know where I was. There was a road going off to the left, so I went running there. I was just going to put myself under this wall but the planes were coming, so I threw myself under a truck instead. The next minute the wall collapsed and the bricks rolled up to me under the truck, so the gods were with me then. There wasn't much left of the convoy, but they started shouting to us to get back on. There was bodies all over the place at the time. There were two Bren-gunners, still hanging on to their guns, and they were obviously dead. There were arms and legs in different places, and it was more like a rubbish heap, spread all over the place. There were stretcher-bearers working but they couldn't cope because they were just picking up limbs. We weren't allowed to help. They just wanted us back on the convoy. You feel hopeless. You feel guilty for leaving it there. The refugees suffered terribly because they were in the road and didn't have chance to get away at all, but we just had to leave them. I didn't think war would be like that. One of the worst things is when you feel some wet on you and you think to yourself you've got some blood there, or you've been hit or something, and what is it? Grey matter. That is really repulsive. It's like the mark of Cain on you for the rest of your life. When you've got somebody's organs spread on you, you don't like it.

As things was going, where the Germans was getting behind us so much, I thought we would have a right ding-dong battle or we would get captured. But you didn't get time to be afraid. You just had to keep going. To a great extent you was waiting for the next rest because we were exhausted, absolutely exhausted, we were right at the end of our tether. Then we went to Cassel. We went into this barn and we strengthened it up a bit, and it was quiet for a while. Then the next minute, up came the Germans. They seemed to pop up all the time but they were easy targets because they used to pop up just like jack-in-the-boxes. Then they started the mortaring. The mortars fell short of the barn, quite a lot of them, but gradually they were knocking it down. We found that you could almost tell where they was going to land, so you always turned the other way. But I got too clever at this. I heard a mortar going up and I thought, 'Right, it's going over there', and I turned away. But it blew the corner of the barn right out and I thought I was blinded. They led me into another room and sent for the stretcher-bearers. Somebody came in and cheered me up by saying, 'What a bloody mess.' But luckily it was brick dust in my eyes and they managed to clean it out. Then the order went out by word of mouth that it would be the last man to the last round. We'd already realised that the situation was hopeless because there was so many Germans round about. And then it became obvious that we were surrounded.

JOE TRINDER

I was the youngest of eleven. My mother had three sons in the First World War and three in the Second. We were a very close-knit family. When the trouble started in 1938, anybody with any common sense knew there was going to be a war. They had meetings in the village hall and we joined the Territorials. I think there was nineteen people out of this village (Bibury, Gloucestershire) that joined the Territorials. To begin with we were just Saturday-night soldiers.

The Glosters' recruitment drive for new members in Bristol, May 1937. *(Courtesy of the Soldiers of Gloucestershire Museum)*

Joe Trinder's wife wasn't going to let Hitler stop her getting married!

Then when war broke out we were all called up and the Bibury platoon went to guard duties at Filton aerodrome. I got married from Filton. They gave me 48 hours to get married. My wife said, 'Well, I don't care if they only give us 12 hours. We're gonna get married. Hitler's not going to stop me getting married.'

In January 1940 we set sail for France. Green as mustard, we were. Half of us hadn't fired a rifle. We landed at Le Havre and went up through the country. We hoped that it would be over quickly, but once we got into France and we saw what we had with us, your mind started to change. I was second-in-command of the transport, and we only had about half a dozen proper army vehicles. The rest was what we called impressed vehicles. They'd gone all round the second-hand merchants and got them. One was a fruit wagon and at one time we had a hearse, but they sent that back. We weren't prepared for war at all. It was terrible, really, to think that we put people up against tanks with rifles.

Of course, it was a terrible winter. Roads were all frozen up and we were sleeping in the wagons, one blanket each. Most of the people were put to digging tank traps on the Belgium border. We stayed there for a month or two and got acclimatised, and then heard we were going to fight in front of the Maginot Line. The old CO was a real First World War man and he was chuffed to death that we were going to scrap but I wasn't very particular about it.

The Germans used to patrol at night and so did we, but most of the time we were in dugouts. We were supposed to be there for a fortnight and we were there for a month. We lost one or two people and they took a few Germans with them. When we came back from the Maginot Line, we had about ten days to get ourselves cleaned up. In that ten days we had a Guards sergeant-major to shake us up together, and he did!

British troops enter the Maginot Line in 1940.

One night, there was a terrible air raid and that was when the Germans started. So we had to load up and get ready. We went back up to the Belgian frontier but they wouldn't let us through, so we pulled up alongside a big wood and at night the birds started singing. There must have been hundreds of nightingales and they were singing like mad. It was beautiful.

Then we went through the Belgian frontier, up towards Waterloo, and we got a peppering. Then we started the trip back, which was dig in, fight, move, dig in, fight and move, all the way back. You'd dig in at night and wait for the morning to have a good go, only to find that the French had gone and you'd got nobody on your right. It was retreat all the time. It was terrible. We got to different places where we really hung in and had a good go, but it wasn't very good. We thought we were gonna stand and have a good scrap. But so many

Following spread: The militia men of the 5th Glosters during the harsh winter of 1940. (IWM F2343)

times you got ready and keyed up to have a go and then you had to retreat and you hadn't fired a shot. It was a sad job, really, all the way through.

There were very often times when I thought I would be killed. You were only inches away from it. We went to one little place and Cookie, my mate, was with me. We were lost from the unit and we were with some RASC (Royal Army Service Corps) chaps. They went out after what the French people said were parachutists, but I don't think they were. I think they were rogue Frenchmen and they were gonna fight for anybody who came along first. Anyway, we cornered them in a field and they fired on us and they killed one of the RASC boys. As soon as they started firing on us, Cookie and me was flat on the floor like a shot. It was winter barley that we got in and the bullets were whipping the tops of the corn off, just over our heads. A bullet makes a funny little noise when it goes by you and I said to Cookie, 'Do you ever pray?' and he said, 'Yeah, sometimes.' 'Well,' I said, 'pray now that that machine-gunner don't get the bloody hiccups, cos if he gets the hiccups, we've had it.' He said, 'How do joke in a state like this?' And I said, 'What else can we do, Horace? We're just here and we take our chance.' There we are.

We went to a small village called Wormhoudt and I started work straight away. They'd had some vehicles shot up and we were trying to make one good one out of two. The transport officer came by and he said, 'Don't worry about them, just smash them up. We're going up to some villages, we'll be there for a few hours, there's about 300 Germans, and we're gonna wipe them up and then we're going hopefully back to England.' Anyway, the next morning we went up to Bruxelle and Ledringhem, all little farm villages. We had orders to hold them for 48 hours, no matter what happened, to allow more BEF to get away from Dunkirk. Well, we spent the night there and the next couple of days weren't too bad. Then we had a spotter plane come over and within minutes we got stonked something terrible. We had 4-inch mortar bombs coming down on us like hail. We could see where the Germans were and instead of 300 I think there were 3,000 there, and they were working their way around these villages.

We had orders to get the vehicles out. There were several burning and we got what we could out and parked them down the road. I was walking back to this little field where there was another vehicle and as I was walking back this voice said, 'Don't leave me, Joey, don't leave me.' But I couldn't see anybody because the grass was long. So I said, 'Where are you?' He said, 'Over in this grass.' So I went over to him and it was Bob Webb. He came from near Bristol somewhere. He was the water cart driver. He was about 20. He said he'd been hit, but that it wasn't hurting. So I moved him and I could see what the problem was. It was terrible. His leg was open from the knee, up the side, right up to his thigh. Just

Truck driver Bob Webb was badly wounded by shrapnel.

laid open as though you'd got a knife and cut it and pulled it apart. And it was cauterised, see, because the shell of course was red hot. Good thing it was too, otherwise he would have bled to death. We pulled his trousers and that away, and cleaned it where the stuff had got in the wound. Had to do it with our hands, we'd got nothing else. You could see the bones all showing up bright white and the veins and everything, muscles twiddling. It was a pretty gruesome sight. It was the first thing (like that) I'd ever seen. But you had to just dig in and get it done. I pulled his clothes away from the wound and tore his trousers right away. I held his leg together and my mate put a field dressing on it. We managed to get him on a Royal Engineers truck and he was on the back, waving as he went. Evidently he got back all right.

FRANK HENN

I'd been given a regular commission in the Gloucestershire Regiment at the end of 1939 after just four months training at Sandhurst and I was 19 when I was given command of a platoon in the 5th Glosters. At the time, of course, one didn't quite realise this to the extent that I realise it now, but one was very inexperienced and really very green indeed. But there was great confidence in an officer in those days, even if he was as young and as green as me. I was very proud to be in the Glosters. Immediately after being commissioned I spent a few weeks at Horfield Barracks in Bristol and all this sort of thing was imbued in you. The Glosters were a very highly regarded county regiment, which received tremendous support within Gloucestershire, and in some ways I think members of the regiment were conscious of the fact that they represented not just the regiment, but Gloucestershire as well.

Frank Henn, shortly after returning from Dunkirk (front row, far left).

My generation was unconsciously brought up to think that Britain, and England, were the best in the world and this flavoured much of one's outlook, so you never thought you could be easily defeated; it just didn't occur to you. Morale was still quite high and in the couple of weeks before our withdrawal from Waterloo we'd never actually been defeated. We'd held successive positions until we were ordered to withdraw, but we were withdrawn at our own volition; we hadn't been driven off by the Germans. And in the one encounter we'd had at the River Escault we'd certainly come off better, so it just didn't occur to you that one might be totally defeated. We were quickly deployed to cover the western flank and the battalion was ordered to deploy forward to two villages: one was called Ledringhem, the other was Arneke. When we got to Arneke, my company commander said I was to take my platoon and hold a position about 2 miles away on a railway embankment. He said this position had to be treated as what was known as a standing patrol position. We were to try to delay any enemy advance along that road and across that railway embankment for as long as possible before rejoining the company. But by then my platoon, which would originally have been about thirty-five men, was down to about ten or twelve.

I had no map, of course, and there was no radio in those days, so I was completely out of touch with the company headquarters, except by what was known as a platoon runner. I was allotted nothing in the way of anti-tank guns, no sappers to crater or mine the road, and nothing with which to block it. We were totally dependent on our small arms, which were light machine guns and rifles. I had no means of calling for artillery fire and of course there was no close air support in those days, so we were out on a very lonely limb. I had no knowledge of who might be on my right or left, certainly no one within view, and I knew nothing of the country, except for what I could see while standing on this embankment.

By then we were all extremely tired having marched long distances with little food and little rest. But I was told I was to impose maximum delay there and that is what I decided we must try and do. The fact that it was virtually an untenable position didn't really occur to me at the time. Frankly, I didn't experience fear. I didn't actually know what we were up against, but it turned out to be the number one SS regiment of the German Army, the SS *Leibstandarte Adolf Hitler* Regiment. If I had known that, I would have been petrified probably. But we certainly didn't think about dying. In fact I saw it as my duty to make sure that my men weren't killed there, that we should withdraw before that happened. One was always brought up on the importance of loyalty to the regiment and loyalty to your men. You just didn't want to let your comrades down.

There was a crossing-keeper's cottage immediately below the embankment and when we arrived there I made that my platoon headquarters. We spent a night there and it was the following day when we saw German dismounted troops advancing towards us in extended order. I remember one of the men saying that there were civilians being driven forward in front of them. I decided that whether that was true or not, we must open fire, which we did and this halted the Germans to our front. But it didn't take long for some of them to work round to a wooded feature which was a little bit higher to our left. I realise now that that is where I ought to have been put, but the Germans worked their way around there and brought fire straight down the railway line. In addition to that, a German spotter aircraft started circling overhead and not only engaged us with a cockpit-mounted machine gun, but was directing either mortar or artillery fire or both on our positions. And as they got round the flank, I realised that the time had come for us to withdraw.

Bill Stanton, the runner whom Frank Henn sent along the railway embankment.

I had one section, which was Bill Stanton's section, about 50 or 60 yards further along the railway line to the right. So I sent a runner across, saying that we were withdrawing and to rendezvous at a barn that was about 200 or 300 yards to our rear. The ground was completely open between where we were and this barn, and I realised that our best chance of getting away from that position was in our platoon truck. When we got on the truck, I discovered that the driver had one arm very badly wounded, so I took over driving because in those days very few men in an infantry platoon were actually able to drive. I drove to this barn where we dismounted and waited for Bill Stanton's section to arrive. I didn't realise it at the time but later someone said to me, 'What has happened to your compass?' We had a compass in a webbing case and when I looked at it, I saw that the compass had been shattered by a bullet, which must have been deflected, so I was very lucky.

At the barn we waited for a little bit. I was lying flat on the ground behind an iron pillar because at that stage we were getting some shelling, which was hitting the barn roof. Bill Stanton arrived – I think he was the only one from his section – and we drove on. Of course I didn't know the way back because I had no map, but at a crossroads another few hundred yards on we came across a Royal Artillery officer and his party. He told me that Arneke itself was now under attack and that we wouldn't be able to return there, so we carried on towards Wormhoudt where I got directed to brigade headquarters. And after holding a position there for about 24 hours, we then set out to march to the coast at Bray Dunes, which is just north of Dunkirk. I can remember the whole thing being very orderly. In due course we were called down to embark in boats and were ferried out to ships, and I came back on a paddle-steamer to Harwich. I think we just lay down wherever we were and slept. I was absolutely whacked.

Frank Henn (right) and Bill Stanton, reunited in France, share their memories of the action at the embankment. *(Courtesy of the* Gloucestershire Echo*)*

There was no sense of shame, and in fact there was a certain pride, both in the 2nd Battalion for their defence of Cassel and the 5th Glosters for the fight that they put up at Ledringhem. Although they were defeats, of course, they weren't quite looked on in that light at the time. I think a certain feeling of comfort was taken from the fact that a very good fight had been put up against very difficult odds. I never thought much more about the action again because there were so many other things going on. But I went out to France a few years ago with the Duke of Gloucester to unveil a memorial and I was asked to take him and his party to the embankment to explain what happened, and then I began think more seriously about it all. Bill Stanton was in the party and I didn't realise it. As I was describing what had happened, a voice spoke up from the back and said, 'Yes, that's quite right,' and this was Bill Stanton. I hadn't seen him after the action until that day.

BILL STANTON

I joined the supplementary reserves before the war. It was a new thing where you served for six months and you were taught soldiering, so if anything happened you became a front-line soldier straight away. As soon as the war was about to start we all got together and had a few beers and a good few laughs in the NAAFI, and we were all thinking what we were gonna do when we got over there. We all thought that the war should happen and that we should go over and stop this nonsense, but at 18, 19, you think you can beat the world and you can't. We thought we'd be back by Christmas, to tell you the truth, but of course we weren't. Not that Christmas anyway.

We went to France and we were up near Lille. From there we went up through the Maginot Line. We had German patrols coming and we had to fight them off. We learnt quite a bit of soldiering there. We learnt when to duck and when to look over the top. We just learnt to be soldiers. We were then sent near Metz and we were training there until about April when they came and told us to pack up our stuff: we were going up to the front. We thought, 'This is good. We're gonna see a bit of action now.' We went up to our position and we dug slit trenches, and by the time we'd got them finished, we were told to pack up again. We were moving back. It was digging in, moving back, and there was no action. Everybody was getting sick and tired of moving, digging in, until we were told that we were going to the River Escault. We went there and held a defensive position, and we had plenty of fighting. It was a grim battle that.

I got my Bren gun on top of this corrugated-iron shed and my number two, Dickie Bird, was lying beside me to change the magazines. Nice fella, he was: little and short and glasses. He was a TA soldier and a good kid, always laughing and joking. We were always joking together. Anyway there was a blown bridge, which we'd blown as we'd come across it. I spotted two men by the bridge dragging things down to the river edge and it was rubber boats. If you're fighting a war, you just wait for the best chance, which is what I did. I waited until they were in the centre of the river and I opened fire. I could see the bullets splashing on the water and people jumping up in the boats and their arms going up in the air and equipment going overboard. Men were jumping or falling into the water. It was the water splashing that made it stand out. At the time I was really in my glory doing it because that was my job. Mortars and artillery and ack-ack guns were firing straight at us to try and silence the gun, but I never even thought about it. Dickie Bird was shouting, 'You got the bastards. Keep it going.' He was bloody patting me on the back all the time.

Bill Stanton watched and waited as the rubber boats crossed the River Escault. *(IWM MH1920)*

He was really feeling good and I was too. Just after that we got the order to withdraw, that we were being replaced by another regiment. We didn't know where we were going, but we ended up at Arneke and Ledringhem.

When we got to Ledringhem, the company commander told Lieutenant Henn that he wanted our platoon to go forward towards the enemy as a standing patrol. There was only about nine of us left. When we got to the railway line, Lieutenant Henn split the platoon up. I think it was five men he kept in the house by the embankment, which was platoon HQ. But to me he said, 'I want you to take a Bren-gun section across on to the railway embankment about a hundred yards down to the right.' From there I could see the main road and all the open fields to the left in front of Henn's position. When I got on to the top of the embankment I found that it was all stones. We couldn't dig any trenches or anything and we just had to lie on the top. I got the Bren gun set up with the barrel pointing over the rails and I thought, 'This'll have to do.' One man I asked to go down to the right-hand side of me, about 20 yards away, to watch the fields on our right because we'd been told the enemy was coming round our flanks, and Dickie Bird stopped with me on the embankment.

All morning we were watching tanks and trucks coming into the village about a mile away across the field. There must have been dozens and dozens of them, so we knew something big was coming. Anyway, I was watching the fields and I saw a line of people coming across. They were civilians; they'd got civilian clothes on. I didn't fire. I let them come across the field and I saw that some of them was carrying rifles. I said, 'No, they're dressed up. They're dressing up Fifth Column.' Anyway, behind them came two lines of men in extended order and they were in full dress uniform, a full-scale frontal attack – at least 100 troops spread out. So I waited and waited until they were in the centre of this field, and when they got into there I started firing left to right and they were dropping. Then the second rank started to run and they were coming to the embankment and I knew we'd had it.

A runner came from Lieutenant Henn to tell me that he was withdrawing and to keep firing. He was pulling off in the truck and that was the best way to get away. I was a bit surprised because I thought we were scoring a real mark on them. I said to Dickie Bird, 'Bloody hell, that's left us in a spot.' And he said, 'Ah well, we'll get back.' Anyway I kept firing. I heard the truck go away on my left and as soon as he'd gone I said to Dickie, 'We're off.' I said to him to go to the fella that I'd put on the right and tell him. But when he went to him he shouted to me, 'He's shot.' So I went over to him and I said to Dickie, 'Get hold of this gun. I'm gonna carry him.' You're told not to help people, but we were getting out of it and I didn't want to leave him there. The Germans would have had him and if you're wounded with the type of German they were, you don't get no hospital treatment. It's just a revolver out and you're dead. So that's why I picked him up and carried him. I carried him for about 200 yards and he kept begging me to put him down, he was in that much pain. So finally I did, I put him down and had a look at him and he'd been shot in the chest. I thought he wasn't going to last long and he didn't. He'd only been down a couple of minutes and he died. So then it was just me and Dickie Bird.

So we went back along this ditch and I knew the enemy were gonna come around the house where Henn had been. One came round on his own and I didn't fire at him; I knew that there was others. If I didn't fire at the first man then they'd come out and I'd probably get a few of them. So he came across the road. He'd got a long coat on and just as he got between 10, 15 feet of us, the others came round the side of the house and I started firing then. This fella that was nearly up to me, he ran to get cover. I got the ones coming round the house and

Bill Stanton.

they went down. I said, 'Dickie, another magazine,' and he was putting another magazine on when I heard a loud crack. Dickie got up, he jumped up and he ran about 10, 15 yards and then dropped. He'd been hit and I don't know what it was but something made him get up. I think it was the shock of being hit. He must have been dead while he was moving because he fell down and when I got to him I looked at him and he was dead. He didn't have a chance. I mean, they were trying to silence the gun and he was at the side of me, so it was probably me that they were after. 'Well,' I thought, 'well, that's me.'

I was lying there firing and I got hit in the jaw. It knocked me out but I don't suppose I was down for long. I could hear them shouting round the house where I'd got these other Germans, and they were being careful about coming round. So I thought, 'This is my time to get out of here.' I was on my own so I picked the gun up and started backing off, watching the road and there was machine guns and rifles firing from all sides. I thought, 'Well, how am I gonna get across this road?' The barn was on my left and the bullets were hitting the corrugated sheeting of this barn and they put the fear of God into me. I ran across the road and when I got to the other side I turned round and fired a couple of bursts behind me to let them know I was still watching. Then I turned round and ran again as fast as I could. There's so many things go through your mind at a time like that. I was newly married and a few weeks before I'd had word that my wife had given birth to a baby girl. I thought I was gonna be killed but I wanted to get back and I was prepared to do anything to get back. I had a feeling that I was gonna do my damnedest to get out of it.

I couldn't see the truck anywhere. I passed the barn and up ahead was a copse on the right-hand side. I thought maybe they'd gone behind the trees. So I made my way along there, stopping and firing a few bursts down the road to cover my back. When I got round the corner I saw the truck still there and those on the back shouted to Henn that I was coming. When I got to the truck they said, 'Where are they?' I said, 'They're both dead. It's only me.' I was covered in blood then. They dragged me on board and Lieutenant Henn drove away. We got to HQ and the man on the truck who was wounded in the arm and myself, we were taken off. There was an ambulance at the HQ and they put us in there. There was two or three other wounded in it and they set off down the road to Dunkirk. From there I got picked up by HMS *Hebe*. I'll never forget it because I got on board and the first thing a sailor said to me was, 'Do you wanna cup of tea?' And I nearly took his hand off getting it. That sticks out, really sticks out. 'Do you wanna cuppa tea, son?'

When I got back to England, my wife and mother came to the hospital to visit. I was that full up emotionally. It was great. The first time I saw my baby, Barbara, was when I came home on leave from the hospital. It was an absolutely marvellous moment when I held her for the first time and I said to her, 'A couple of weeks ago I thought I'd never be here to see you.' It was a wonderful feeling. You can't describe it. I wanted to eat her and I felt that I'd got something nobody else had got. A lot of my mates wouldn't get back. You think to yourself, 'I'm here, I'm seeing them again. How on Earth did I do it?'

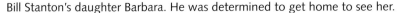

Bill Stanton's daughter Barbara. He was determined to get home to see her.

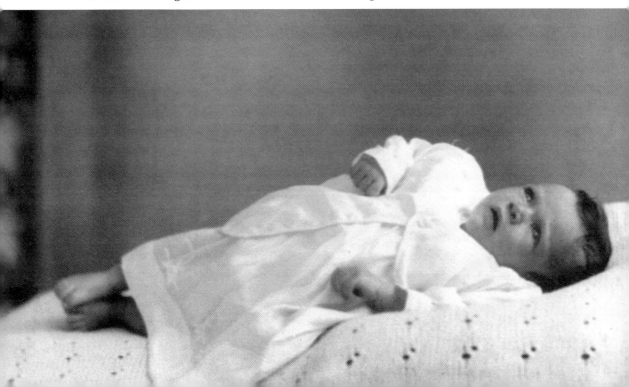

The thing that gets at me is not being able to find Dickie Bird's grave. Of course, we know now that the Germans used to chuck the bodies in any ditch and just cover them over, but I've been over there many, many, many times, looking in cemeteries and everywhere, but I can't find him. I've looked in the ditches and the roadsides to see if I could see any signs of a grave or anything like that. So his body must be lying somewhere, unmarked. I feel rough about that. I've walked my legs off round cemeteries to try and find him. Those things they stick in your mind. Your mates and the ones that you can't help, and you've got to leave them there.

JIM LOFTUS

My father was the Permanent Staff Instructor in the Glosters and when I was 14 I joined the 4th Battalion of the regiment as a band boy, playing the oboe and the band flute. After I had been in the band two years the bandmaster said I was tone deaf and couldn't play a note. My brother was a drummer in the Royal Berkshire Regiment and when he came home in all his regalia I decided to run away from home and join the regular Army. I joined the Marines and the Royal Berkshire Regiment. Eventually I was switched to the Glosters and I never looked back.

When war broke out, the mood was good. We did drill round the main square with a pick and shovel, with the band playing. We were stationed at Seaton Barracks in Plymouth. When we left for France we thought we would be home by Christmas because propaganda had it that Morris Minors were hitting the German tanks and the tanks were collapsing. But to me, the regular soldiers of the German Army were far superior to us.

From the time when we were in France – it was the severest winter of the war, I would have thought – we spent the time digging, digging and digging. We had no kit to offset the cold or the wet. And the following day, with your boots muddied up to the ankles, you'd be told that some VIP was coming out and that we had to be properly clean when they came out. We were still polishing brass buttons and boots right until the Blitzkrieg started in May.

My unit was the brigade anti-tank unit. We had a 25mm Hotchkiss gun carried on a Bedford 15-hundredweight truck and it was supposed to fire a 1-pound shell. If you went into action there were two ramps on the side and you gotta take the ramps off, unhook the gun, lower the gun on to the ground, get into action, open the legs out, load a pound shell and you're ready. It took a long time. The quickest we ever did it was 2½ minutes. But the German tanks, they were already loaded. When the Blitzkrieg started on 10 May we organised to go

Jim Loftus remembers the constant digging. *(IWM O425)*

into Belgium and on the way up the Belgian people welcomed us in. They were coming out, clapping us, shouting and giving us drinks and food. I was in a Bedford truck and I had more champagne than I've ever seen on my truck. Flowers, chocolates – you name it, we had it on the truck. We were elated. No worry at all. The following morning we had the French retreating through us, the Belgians retreating through us, and we were left on our own. After about 24 hours of this, the powers that be told us to retreat. And as we moved back, the Belgian people who praised us on the way in, booed us on the way out. I hated them. How can you change from goodness to badness in 48 hours?

When we left Waterloo, we had to come through a town called Tournai and it was quite a big town. But our main route was blocked with people with their horses and carts, moving away from the Germans. And this is where the Stukas hit us. I was frightened. You could see these black things coming over, diving. You could see the bombs falling. They told me afterwards that if you can see the bomb

Above: The Glosters were welcomed as they moved into Belgium to meet the advancing Germans. Within hours they would begin the withdrawal towards Dunkirk. *(IWM O69)*

falling, it's not gonna hit you. I don't believe it. I was more scared of that than anything. To be blown to pieces. You can't honestly relive it without feeling upset. We lost a third of the battalion, killed or wounded, in that strafing. It was atrocious. It was awful to see – not just the military side, but all these people diving for cover, horses dead. I saw lots of dead bodies, but you couldn't tell if they were soldiers or civilians. It was littered and we had to get out of it. I was sat in the front of my truck and we deviated away from the main road. We cut across country, driving through hedges, and picked up about 2 miles further down the road, so we were in front of the convoy. We got orders then that we were to go to Dunkirk, but that was rescinded and we were told to go to Cassel to fight the rearguard.

When we got to Cassel the Stukas had just hit and there were dead horses all around, so we had to tow the dead horses to one side as the battalion came through. Companies were put out at various positions around the town and my domain was at a place called Zuytpeene, at the bottom of the hill. The CO at Zuytpeene ordered that the nine Bren-gun carriers go out on a listening patrol taking one artillery gun with them, and that was mine. The carrier sergeant stopped and waved me up. He told me to go up the road, turn left and left again and see what happened. So we went along and we were confronted with two tanks. We got off the truck, got the ramps down, got the gun off the truck and started to load the ammunition. But we had only loaded one round when the tanks hit us. They blew the gun to pieces and the truck was riddled. I was just by the side of the gun but wasn't harmed at all. We hid in a ditch where there was a lot of mud and water and I just lay there. I've never seen so many bullets coming towards me. I just buried my face in the ground and every one missed. About 10 minutes later I heard somebody coming towards me so I peeped up and it was a Frenchman coming from one of the houses, so we ran across to his home.

When I got back to Cassel, I was told to join up with the Ox and Bucks Regiment, who were in the town with us, and they had a gun opposite the cemetery. You have an awful job firing a rigid barrel gun at someone coming up a hill because you can't depress it enough to hit them. But they had managed to depress the gun and they scored four direct hits which stopped the German tanks. Our company commander was a chappie by the name of Captain Dixie and he wanted to have a go on the gun. He was 6 feet tall and as he stood up a bullet hit him in the back of the head; he was dead. Let's face it, I was 20 and to see a man, a friend, dead as quick as that, it upset me.

LEN LLEWELLYN

I was 21 in 1939 and within three weeks of my birthday and finishing my apprenticeship with the Gas Board. I was called up to report to Colston Street (Bristol) to go in the Army. I thought it was gonna be an adventure. I wasn't scared or anything like that.

I was a fit person, but I was a bit finicky with my food. My father was a Guardsman, and I can always remember him saying to me, 'Whatever there is to eat, even if you don't like it, eat it, it'll always do you good.' The medical officer who examined me in Colston Street said I was the fittest person he'd examined. I had a chest expansion of 5 inches. This was because as a child I'd had TB and I was in a convalescent home for a twelve month, and all the treatment was exercise and fresh air. The breathing exercises expanded my chest and I was like a pocket Hercules. I played water polo for the Gas Board and I had a couple of games for Bristol City, filling in when they were short. I did go to Broad Weir swimming baths every Sunday morning with my two

Opposite: The deadly Stuka dive-bomber, which caused so much damage at Tournai. *(IWM GER18)*

The 2nd Glosters at Seaton Barracks, 1938. *(Courtesy of the Soldiers of Gloucestershire Museum)*

sisters and we used to play water polo before breakfast. Anyway after about two weeks, I was told to report to Horfield Barracks, which was just up the road on the tram car from me. I spent three months training and after my training I went to France to join the 5th Glosters. At that time they were at the Maginot Line.

It didn't enter my head to consider if the war would be over in three months or six months or three years; I had no idea how long it would take. I was there for about two weeks, then we were withdrawn for a rest. While we were resting the balloon went up and the Germans came round at Belgium. At that time we were sent up to engage them. On getting up to their line, I remember we were in a ditch at the side of the road, a platoon of us of about twenty: ill-equipped, no radio, no map, no compass, no machine guns, nothing like that. Our officer had left us. He might have had a map but we'd lost him. And we were engaging the enemy across a field, no more than 100, 150 yards. If we had had binoculars, we could have seen where they were, but we couldn't. All you could see was the machine gun spouting fire every now and again. They had a fixed line on a farm gate that was open. We were trying to get past this farm gate and every time

Below: Exhausted troops from the Belgian Army on the retreat. *(IWM F4483)*

you showed yourself, they fired. Well, eventually we all separately made a dash across the gate and from that time on, we was lost. That began our walk down to Dunkirk.

Now, the way down to Dunkirk took more or less a week and we had to scavenge for food. The only food that I had was what I call a mangoldwurzel. It was like a big swede, cattle food, but that lasted me for three days. I found it in a field. There were no more, just this one swede. It was quite a large thing, about 6-inch diameter all the way round, and I cut that up with a penknife. I wouldn't say it was delicious or anything, but it was something to chew on, and it was something going in your body, to keep your body working. It was like my father said, as long as you got something in your stomach, you were all right.

I think I must have been walking in my sleep half the time: we never stopped to go to sleep because the Germans were right behind us. At one time we were turning right and they began shelling, so we made a detour about a mile down the road and they lengthened their range. The shells exploded near enough to us to cover us with soil but we were lucky that there was no shrapnel. I had a pal I was with and he panicked. He threw off his equipment and ran to the roadway. I ran after him and when I caught up with him he was on a horse, trying to get the horse to go. But the horse was exhausted and I suppose it hadn't had anything to eat, so I got him down and we continued our walk down to Dunkirk.

The roads were filled with vehicles that had run out of petrol and had been abandoned. Of course, on the way down we were strafed all the way. Every time they came and dive-bombed, as I call it, we did jump into the ditch. At one time I jumped into a hedge and caught hold of a chap. I was behind him and I had my hands on his shoulders and I said, 'That was a near one.' I turned him round and half of his face was missing. It had been blown off and he was obviously dead. Terrible that was. I just jumped up and I ran from him.

Men were falling out with their feet turning raw. The heavier they were, the worse their feet got. I remember big, tall chaps, they just sat down on the road and they couldn't go any further. There was a chap from St George and he just sat down on the side of the road; he was taken prisoner of war. I felt dreadful. It was just like running away, but we had no option. We didn't have the equipment to make a stand. They were advancing with armoured vehicles and we were just on foot. They were just a couple of miles behind you all the way down.

TWO

DUNKIRK

The Glosters' Great Escape

The 5th Battalion of the Glosters held their positions in the villages of Arneke and Ledringhem for four days before the order to withdraw was received on 28 May 1940. By this time the men were completely surrounded, and with German infantry beginning to break into Ledringhem it took several bayonet charges, made to the gallant cry of 'Up the Glosters', to drive the enemy from the village and allow the battalion to escape. This scene was graphically captured in an article printed in the *Gloucester Citizen* on 15 June 1940 written by Lieutenant Michael Shephard, who took part in the charge. Casualties had been heavy and those too injured to leave were left behind, attended by two medical orderlies. But by 00.15 hours on 29 May the 5th Glosters were at last making their way to Dunkirk. En route they captured a small number of German prisoners before stopping to rest in the village of Bambecque, which was being held by the 8th Worcesters. According to regimental records, the adjutant of the Worcesters wrote, 'During the early morning stand-to I saw a wonderful sight. Round the corner as I came out of Battalion HQ appeared the survivors of the 5th Gloucesters. They were dirty and haggard, but unbeaten. Their eyes were sunken and red from lack of sleep, and their feet as they marched seemed to me no more than an inch from the ground. At their head limped a few prisoners. . . . I ran towards Colonel Buxton (the CO), who was staggering along, obviously wounded. I took Colonel Buxton indoors . . . assuring him again and again that his men were all right.'

By 31 May some 400 men from the 5th Battalion had been evacuated from Bray Dunes. During their time in France, two officers and eighty-five men had been killed and many more wounded. But the battalion had proved itself in the field of battle and won one Military Cross and seven Military Medals.

German troops advancing through a village in Northern France. *(IWM MH13134)*

At Cassel, the 2nd Battalion was also being surrounded and it too should have received the order to withdraw on 28 May. Unfortunately, the despatch rider carrying the message was unable to get through the lines and the besieged battalion was forced to fight on for a further 24 hours before the order was eventually received; it probably goes without saying that this delay had catastrophic consequences. By the time the 2nd Battalion began its escape Cassel was in flames and the hillside town was completely encircled. Fleeing under cover of darkness, the exhausted men made their way into a large wood, the Bois St Acair, which is situated on the left-hand side of the road leading to Dunkirk. Shortly afterwards the battalion, including Julian Fane, Jim Loftus and Bill Lacey, found themselves trapped in the wood. Under heavy mortar fire and in the ensuing chaos 137 men were killed and 484 taken prisoner. For those lucky enough to escape, the route to the coast was fraught with danger and it took great skill, courage and good fortune to evade capture, or worse.

For their actions in France, and in particular the defence of Cassel, the 2nd Glosters were awarded two Military Crosses, one Distinguished

GLO'STERSHIRE BATTALION'S EPIC FIGHTS IN FLANDERS

(4)

HOW THE SURVIVORS ESCAPED TO THE COAST

Men Very Fatigued

Many of the men were very fatigued and stunned by the shelling we had endured so long, and for a while they would be of little use in defending H.Q. Others had received slight wounds which had to be dressed; more men were engaged in dressing the wounded in the yard behind H.Q.

We did not feel that we could withdraw more men from the posts which were now under fire. Yet there was the very necessary fact that the enemy must be driven out of the village before any attempt at withdrawal could be made. With enemy on every side a withdrawal is certain to fail once it becomes a running fight.

Therefore, seven officers and seven men with rifles and bayonets and a few hand grenades and two men with Bren guns prepared to attack the enemy 150 yards away. We waited against the wall of the H.Q. and in the ditch on the other side of the road. Then we spread out and began moving slowly down the street.

I expect every man there felt the same as I did—not frightfully brave, doing it because it was absolutely essential that it should be done, wondering whether it would hurt when it came and taking courage and hope from the presence of the others.

Their War Cry

It was natural that we should take to some kind of war-cry ("Up Gloucesters") and shout encouraging words to each other, at the same time gaining confidence as we moved forward.

Our pace increased but we did not break into a run for it was necessary to keep a look out for any enemy who might be lingering further up the street than we expected.

The burning houses cast an eerie glow against the church walls and proved of assistance to us for we were able to see the Germans cross the street ahead of us. They gave us a rather feeble volley which was returned wholeheartedly by our rifles fired from the hip—and on we went. When we reached the bottom of the street, the Germans were quiet.

The enemy had established a machine-gun at the corner by the church and were worrying us again with their tommy-guns. This time we had more men; reinforcements had come to us from posts where they could be spared. Two more officers were with us and most of the men were those who had been on fighting patrols in France—the very medicine for the Boche.

I think the German officer must have sensed that we meant business this time; we could hear him exhorting his men to meet our attack.

Cold Steel

The first sense of fear had left is and it was almost thrilling moving down that street to get to grips with those grey clad infantrymen. So, cheering, thirty odd men and officers moved steadily towards the corner by the church. The blaze had grown greater and we could see the figures of the enemy as they waited in the cover of walls and doorways. The light of his making showed us the leader who was shouting harshly to his men. I saw him at the same time that others did and simultaneously our rifles cracked and the German went down.

Admittedly, we lost men as we went forward, but that was to be expected, and did not seem to deter the others.

Suddenly the road was illuminated by great explosions as the enemy rolled and threw their stick-bombs at us.

Our own grenades replied, and one, neatly lobbed through a doorway, silenced the machine gun for good. We fired another volley at the shadowy figures and then—— We ran in.

On my right I saw a Tommy bayonet a man. I heard him shout triumphantly and by his voice it was the Welshman again.

Another Tommy ran past me and round the corner to bayonet a Boche who crouched there with his bombs. Another German ran away from that place and fell at my feet before I realised that I had fired again from the hip. Everywhere our men were doing the same thing—bayoneting, shooting and bombing. Everywhere we were pushing the enemy back from the village.

It was exhilarating.

For a moment we withdrew a few yards to collect ourselves for the final assault. The two Brens were brought up to cover us.

The Germans were again rolling bombs towards us from cover and it was one of these which, bursting some distance away, gave me a slight wound by the eye. It was not much, hurt not the slightest, but blinded me with blood for the moment. So I gave my bombs to someone or other and went back to have my face dressed.

While I went back the others went forward again and by the time I had been patched up the street was quiet.

We lost several officers and men, dead and wounded, in that rush; but the object had been achieved. We were more or less free to go.

Many of us had received scratches, from the Colonel down to the Private; but our tails were higher than they had been an hour before.

Still a Battalion

Half an hour afterwards the advanced guard left the village, crawling through the long grass past the windmill where the enemy had a machine-gun post and following our route along the streams.

An hour later the rear-guard caught us up and we carried on back through the German lines, picking up a German officer and some men as prisoners on the way and passing several bunches of the enemy asleep in the grass. We let sleeping Boche lie.

It was amusing to be asked by the German officer whether we were a "crack" British Regiment?

We certainly had the best of the German Army in that push against the French and the B.E.F.—their motorised divisions and their shock troops and S.S. Men.

So it was that early in the morning after breaking back from the village in which the Germans had hoped to trap us, the Gloucesters marched through the Worcester outposts as a Battalion—a tired and tattered and greatly reduced Battalion, but as a Battalion for all that.

The bayonet charge at Ledringhem, graphically described in Michael Shephard's article, which appeared in the *Gloucester Citizen* in June 1940.

Conduct Medal and eleven Military Medals, including one for Julian Fane. The brigadier, Somerset, was subsequently made a CBE and the commanding officer, Lieutenant-Colonel Gilmore, received the Distinguished Service Order. Both Julian Fane and Jim Loftus were Mentioned in Despatches. But these awards came at a price: only around 100 men from the 2nd Battalion made the great escape back to England.

The last stand made by the Gloucestershire Regiment during the withdrawal to Dunkirk is just another in its long line of military achievements. Although the bravery of the Royal Navy and the fleet of little ships has entered national folklore, the heroic defence of the perimeter, at villages and towns like Ledringhem and Cassel, is often overlooked. But the sacrifice of the Glosters helped delay the German advance to Dunkirk and as a consequence 338,000 British and French soldiers made it to British soil, ready to fight another day.

JULIAN FANE

The order to retreat came on 29 May. I think they'd tried to get through to us earlier but were unable to do so. Eventually a despatch rider did reach us and we heard that we were to withdraw to Dunkirk. We withdrew company by company into the flat plain. It was dark and being summer of course it didn't get dark until 10 o'clock. The town was in flames, smoke everywhere, and we just filtered away. We were told to make for a large wood on the left as we made our way to Dunkirk. There must have been two or three companies in this wood and we took up defensive positions during the night. Very soon we heard the Germans crying out in English, saying, 'You are surrounded. Come out with your hands up or we'll shell you out.' I was reminded of stories which I'd heard where people had been told to come out and had all been shot dead, so we just stuck where we were. Then they started shelling, and shelling in woodland is not very pleasant because the shells tend to burst in the trees at head height and shrapnel spreads much more than if it just lands with a plomp and makes a hole in the ground. So we then decided to move to another part of this very large wood and on the word go we dashed across. Of course we were machine-gunned as we went. A few people were hit and fell. I landed up in a gorse bush on the other side, but eventually most of us got across unscathed.

I suppose we were in the wood for a whole day. Then as darkness fell we were given instructions to make our way out, company by company. We were about 20 yards away from a large hedge in a field of about 20 acres, a very big field, in the middle of which was a haystack. As we moved forward, the whole of the hedge and the haystack were set ablaze by rifle fire, mortars and grenades. We fell to the ground and I remember turning towards the fire and burying my face in the mud. I was very lucky because a mortar bomb landed straight in front of my head. One part of it glanced off my tin hat and the other part wounded me in the arm, but I only realised I was wounded when the warm blood was dripping down my arm. But, I mean, if I hadn't had my tin hat on, they would have called time for me. I was obviously very frightened indeed. You would be if you were surprised, ambushed by superior firepower and with no means of replying. But it's amazing what the human body will withstand if the mind is there to drive it, and one still had in one's mind not to give in: one had to escape. Something had to be done to avoid dying. That's the thing that drives you on. You don't just give in.

At that point I wondered whether there was anything we could do to counter-attack but I realised there was no possibility at all. I knew that in front of me was a lieutenant, Olive was his name, and he was hit in the chest and died. There was a quarter-master sergeant called Farmer who was also hit. He had a bandolier around his shoulders and that was hit and the bullets were all flying from it. The haystack was still illuminated and so we were between the devil and the deep blue sea. We had a marvellous light behind us and the enemy on our left. I thought we'd better make for some better cover than this because we were just lying out in the open. I crawled forward and found my sergeant, White, and he was dead. I went further on until I got to a road which ran across the top of the field and jumped into a ditch. I was rather irritated because there were many more people in the ditch and I was on top, so I was exposed and I thought that was a bad thing! I moved further along and found a deeper ditch.

I collapsed into this ditch, I must admit. I discovered there were one or two other people there – one excellent man called Corporal Eldridge and he had two hand-grenades. I had a pistol and a few rounds of ammunition. And there was another private there called Lacey, who had a rifle, so that was our total armament. Lacey then kindly put a dressing on to my arm. Of course a wound like that swells up and your whole arm goes like a balloon. I began to get afraid of getting blood poisoning and all that sort of stuff but there was nothing you could do, so you just carried on.

I then decided with Corporal Eldridge that we should move on and try to get through the German lines. We knew that the defensive position at Cassel was to cover the withdrawal to Dunkirk, so we knew we had to get to the coast. It was merely a question of how we did it. I started off with twelve men. I told them to come with us and we would lead them through, hopefully.

After crossing a number of fences and a stream or two, I decided we would have to take cover before daylight. We were all rather wet and we shared what rations we had. I had a loaf of bread, which I shared out. We all took our boots off because our feet were swelling, had a bite to eat, smoked a cigarette and had a little bit of a rest. We spent the day there under cover and we knew there was German activity nearby – looking out you could see the road and you could see German traffic going up and down.

Come the evening I heard a horse-drawn artillery convoy moving down this road, away from Dunkirk, and I thought to myself, 'This must be a French horse-drawn battery because surely the Germans wouldn't have gone so far so fast without mechanised artillery?' I told everybody to be quiet and I chanced my arm. I climbed cautiously out of the ditch and I walked slowly across a field of turnips to get to the side of the road. Leading this convoy was a man on a bicycle. I asked him in French what he was doing and whether he had just come back from Dunkirk. The chap on the bicycle replied in German: 'I don't speak French!' So I saluted smartly, thanked him, bowed my head and walked slowly back across the field, hoping not to get a bullet in the back! Although I was in full battledress, tin helmet, everything, I don't think he realised I was British. I think he thought I was French. But I think they were all tired and exhausted, so they went on and I went on.

We stayed in the ditch the following day and then come the evening I decided we should make for the nearby town of Oost-Cappel. The first big house on the left was the post office. We went in and I found a calendar on the wall which was rather helpful because it showed a map of Northern France. We found some food and wine and were very happy dug in there. Come 1am I had great difficulty telling the guys that we were going to move on, but we couldn't sit around. So we got on and I made my way across country. As I took them along a path by a copse suddenly I saw looming up in front of me some black shapes. We all took cover, threw ourselves on the side of the path, and four German tanks rolled by. I thought they were going to crush my feet.

Daylight was coming on and I knew we had to find somewhere to take cover. I found a big farmhouse with a large outbuilding and decided we would go in there. It was a typical farm building with straw and hay on both sides and open carts in the middle. There was a ladder on the right up to the straw, so I got everybody up there and we baled the straw one on top of the other to give us a bit of cover. We settled down, nice and warm, nice and dry. No smoking, no talking, no sneezing, no nothing. I then heard German soldiers down below in the yard. Suddenly, a face appeared over the top of the ladder and looked at us. It was the farmer. Corporal Eldridge put his finger to his lips and said, 'Ssshhh.' The farmer nodded and clambered down the ladder. We just had to pray that he didn't say anything. Anyway, he remained silent, which was brave of him, because if they'd discovered us he might have copped it.

Eventually we heard the Germans drive away. We made our way onwards as soon as it was dark, guided really by the flash of the guns and the burning farmhouses, which the Germans set alight to show the positions of their forward troops. We were going through a position which was amongst some trees and it all seemed very quiet so I walked forward. Suddenly Corporal Eldridge said, 'My God, sir, hold on.' I was just about to step on a German who was dug into a little trench, asleep! We wondered whether or not we should kill him, but I thought it would make too much noise so we all stepped over this wretched chap in turn and went on.

Eventually we came to a large canal, which was at least 20 feet wide. Some of the chaps couldn't swim and my arm had blown up by this time so I wasn't in swimming order really. Then we found a boat which had been partly sunk on the other side. Corporal Eldridge volunteered to swim across, very cold water too. He tied a string to a bit of rope and brought it back across to us. I discovered a large REME (Royal Electrical and Mechanical Engineers) lorry with large trays in it, tools and things, so I emptied all that out and used the trays to put people in and ferry them across. We got across and just as we did we heard some bullets from behind. Then a farmer came out of a house and said the Germans hadn't crossed the canal, so we were thankful about that. On we went.

We went by daylight now and didn't bother about having to skulk because I didn't think we were in the German lines. Eventually we came across the sea at De Panne. There was a rough coast road, not very broad, and then the beaches. We saw ships standing off and we saw people on the beaches, but we left them and we walked about a mile towards Dunkirk, which was my aim. You could see Dunkirk because it was pouring black smoke where the oil tanks had been set alight. A lot of the houses were in flames. Still, that was my object: get to Dunkirk.

When we got to the outside of the town, there was a row of cottages and the very first cottage we came to was empty so I put all the guys into a room on the left and they took their packs off. I then left them in there and went to the front door. I was in the doorway wondering what to do next when a bomb fell very close to the house. The walls of the house collapsed in on me and then went out

British troops were still under threat once they had reached Dunkirk. *(IWM FX7529)*

again. I was shot out like a bullet out of a gun. I was trying to work out what to do for the guys but I was then swished on to the mole before I could say anything. People were saying, 'Come on, get on, get on!' I was dragged on really and was put on to a submarine chaser. Realising I could do nothing more, realising that I couldn't go back, I collapsed and went to sleep. I didn't wake up until I got to Dover. What I worried about was that I had somehow deserted my men in this bloody building, which had collapsed, presumably on them. I always felt frightfully guilty and worried about them.

When I came off the ship and down the gangplank I was whisked on to an ambulance train. The carriages had stretchers on either side and I was looking out of the window, which I could see very clearly because I was lying down flat, and I suddenly saw the most extraordinary sight. I mean, some 20 miles away from me we'd been in absolute hell and suddenly there were men in white flannels on very carefully mown turf playing cricket and further along there were girls in white shorts and white shirts all playing tennis, as if nothing had happened. It was like leaving hell and arriving in heaven.

Bill Lacey was on the run with Julian Fane for about a week before they finally reached the coast.

BILL LACEY

On the last day in Cassel we got moved out of the barn to fire everything that we'd got down on a convoy that was going by. Then when it became dusk, we found some piglets and the cooks cooked them. There's always someone who says something wrong: when we were eating in the dark someone said, 'It's the Last Supper.' Then about midnight we went out. But I think, really, the majority of us would have rather stopped there and died than have gone out that night. We knew we were surrounded and we accepted it. And we were there, last man, last round, as they said. But it didn't happen.

Dawn was coming and the Germans drove us into a wood. They were firing and they put mortar bombs in. They even used a tank at one time. Then they was going around, asking us to come out, that we were friends and that we'd be treated properly. I believe that there was a small party of the Glosters went out and they were killed. They (the Germans) were firing into the woods all the time so we had to wait until dusk and then we moved out again. Then, I don't know if it was the second or the third night, they booby trapped the area. We got to a road with a ditch alongside and they (the officers) said they wanted someone to cross the road to get to the ditch on the other side. I was one of the first up and no sooner did we get into the middle of the road than all hell broke loose.

I threw myself into the ditch and it was pretty shallow, about 2½ feet deep, and the bodies was falling on top of you, people was crying out. The tracer bullets were flying over and a haystack had been set alight. That was carnage there. You couldn't raise your head up at all. All you could do was to crawl along, crawl over bodies and things like that. Then we went right up to the end and there was another trench going up to the left. I got into the side there and it was just like being in heaven, no firing at all. There was about fourteen or sixteen of us. Then we found an officer in amongst us – Julian Fane. He took charge from then on. He had been hit and I looked at it. I noticed that he had red streaks up his arm and I thought, 'Crikey, he's in for gangrene.' I put a field dressing on but I had to do it very gently because it was obvious that there was shrapnel in it. There was nothing we could do there, only wait to be captured, so we moved off and we was on the run from then on.

I was with Julian Fane all the way back to Dunkirk. Whoever is senior takes command and he was well worthy of the job. Although he was wounded, he kept his calm. It took us nearly a week to get down to Dunkirk and we had to dodge the Germans all the way. He had no compass and he had no maps and he was trying to go by the stars and things like that. But our movements were dictated by where the Germans were. All we had to do was to avoid being captured. But he led the way, all the way, and we just followed.

When we got to Dunkirk, we went into this big building there and I thought that Julian had gone into the first aid place. The rest of us was in this house having a rest. But no sooner did we get in than the Military Police came and was turfing everybody out. As we left, the planes was coming over. We threw ourselves on the sand and the next minute the building came down, so we got away with that one too.

We was all split up then and there was hundreds on the beach. I joined a party and we tried to get a raft out but the planes came over and two more got killed. They couldn't swim so when the planes came over they didn't duck under the water as we did and they got killed on the raft. Anyhow, I got back on to the beach. You could see the mole and the planes were still coming over and I thought, 'I'm not going to get anywhere here at all.' But someone grabbed hold of me and says, 'Come on, get going.'

I was in the queue to get on this boat and there were some wounded there, so I gave up my place and joined the rearguard in the town. But the Germans were everywhere and men were giving themselves up as prisoners, so I made a run for it. I was on the run for four months and didn't come home until October. I had to find my own food: one day I found a tin, which I thought was beetroot. I was really slavering as I opened it but it was just margarine. But it wasn't too bad spread on some straw. I couldn't wear my uniform, so I found some civilian clothes, but it was getting cold, and if I got wet, I couldn't dry out. If I'd been there any longer, I would have had to have given myself up.

I thought I'd walked all over France and the Germans were after me all the way. They would have shot me if they'd found me. Eventually I went back to

Many Allied troops were left behind following the evacuation. *(IWM HU2287)*

Dunkirk and I stole a fishing boat. I left the harbour and a German spotlight came on me, but they must have seen the boat before because they switched it off again. When I got to England, I had trouble proving my story but I was reported in all the French newspapers, so I had proof.

We were defeated. There's no doubt about that. The ones that won was the boats, the small boats and the Navy. As far as the Army was concerned, we were absolutely defeated. Thing was, they weren't treating us as a defeated army. They were treating us as heroes but we weren't. The funny part about it was that once we got home, although there was talk about us being invaded by the Germans, nobody ever thought that they would succeed. And everybody had the feeling that we would be back one day. Don't know where, don't know when, as they say.

It's meant a lot to me to be reunited with Julian Fane. I never thought I'd see him again. He's someone I look up to and it's something that I boast about now, actually – to be able to say I've met someone that was with me at the time. It's the spirit of the Glosters, I suppose.

Bill Lacey (right) and Julian Fane share their memories, finally reunited after over sixty years.

JOE TRINDER

We were told to leave the village (Ledringhem) so we got the last two vehicles out. We went about three quarters of a mile and we came to a T-junction. I didn't know what the hell to do. The Warwicks or the Worcesters had formed a roadblock there and I said to the officer, 'Will you let us through so that we can get these vehicles back to our unit?' He said, 'If you go through there, up on the corner there's the Germans. They've cut the road behind your people so you can't get back. If you poke you're head round that corner you'll get your brains blown out.' He said, 'Your best plan, Corporal, is to get your men, get them on a vehicle and make for Dunkirk.' So that's what we did. But the others left at the villages, they held them for 48 hours, then for another 12 and another 12. Then they were told they could get out, but by that time there was no way out. The old CO, he led a bayonet charge through the village, waving his pistol. 'Up the Glosters,' he said. They just fixed their bayonets, they went down through the village like a load of locusts and they routed the Jerry out of the village. They did that twice.

Joe Trinder (middle) didn't think he would ever see home again.

When we got into Dunkirk – well, we got to De Panne actually – we used to go down on the coast every evening and shout 'Ship ahoy' like hell, hoping to attract some attention, but we didn't see a boat. Then we made our way into Dunkirk and by that time there were queues right out to sea, about three queues and we joined one of them. Every time someone was taken off on a boat, it meant another step or two forward for you. It was all right for those that had water up to their middle but me being a bit short, I had water up to my chest. We stuck it all one night and we were soaking wet through. I said to my friend, 'This is not for me. I'm gonna find another way home and it's just too bad if we get took.' Anyway, we got out and in the dunes, out of the way. We dried ourselves when the sun came out in the morning. Every time we stayed anywhere we used to dig a hole. I think I dug twenty holes on Dunkirk beach with the blasted mess tin. That's all we had to dig with. Blokes were scratching holes out with their hands, just to get below ground, because you were being strafed every day. The old Stukas were coming over and bombing us like hell. Anyway, we hunted around but the east mole wasn't working at that time: it had been shelled and great big holes had been blown in it.

British troops wade out to freedom. The sea was too deep for Joe Trinder. *(IWM HU1528)*

Many like Joe Trinder hid in the dunes to escape the threat of dive-bombers. *(IWM HU 1528)*

I didn't think we would get away because at times it came to a complete standstill. I've heard people say that people were rioting and they were fighting to get on the boats but I never see a thing like that. Every man that I see on that beach was cool as cucumber. They never lost their wits at all. They were doing their best to get away, naturally, but I didn't see any panic. We had no proper food. We had emergency rations and we broke into them – chocolate and stuff like that – and it used to keep you going. You'd break a bit off, have a little square. If you did come across a body, and there was plenty about, you'd just look through the pockets and see if they'd got any packs of biscuits or anything like that in there. Some had, some hadn't. But we found odds and ends about that kept us going. One night we found a house that was still standing. It was no good getting inside because of the bombing and all that. I slept in the front porch. My feet was up against one wall, my head was up the other end. Even as short as I am there wasn't room to stretch out. I had a beautiful night's sleep and in the morning somebody shook me up and said, 'Corporal, I've brought your breakfast,' and he gave me a hard biscuit. Where he'd got it from I don't know, but I ate it and it was just like bacon and eggs for me!

It's hard to explain the thoughts that went through your head when you see where somebody had made an effort to bury somebody and his feet was sticking out the bottom. You thought, 'Am I going to be like that?' It was pretty haggard really. But there we are, you had to accept this kind of thing. It was war. Although this may sound a bit ambiguous, I was never, ever afraid and I think 90 per cent weren't: they were scared, a little bit scared, but never afraid. Because if you started to be afraid, you did stupid things and made the wrong decisions in your head. Other people were relying on you and you had to keep reminding yourself of that.

We were on the beach about four days. Then we heard they were repairing the east mole and the Navy were organising things. Before you could get on, you had to get a serial number. I think mine was 509. They wanted you to get into parties of fifty and you went up and up. There was a guard of Guardsmen and they wouldn't let anybody pass who didn't have a serial number. Anyway, our number came up and we got to the mole. We got to the foot of it and the old commander was sat up on top on a shooting stick. When the shells went over, he'd duck his head. The old Jerry was very particular; he used to keep to time and you could tell when the next salvo was due, so after the next salvo came over the commander would shout, 'Up! Now run like bloody hell.' There was a matelot at the end of the mole and he was holding the boat in. I was last because I was corporal and I made sure everybody got up. It was an old cross-Channel boat and I don't know where they'd dug him up from, I'm sure. I think it was only the rust that was holding him together.

There was a 6-inch plank running from the mole through a hatchway on the boat. The matelot said, 'Down here, Tommy,' and I said, 'How the bloody hell do I get down there?' He said, 'Slide down the plank.' I had a rifle and I looked and there was all the bodies floating down underneath. I thought, 'There's no way I'm gonna join them', so I slid down the plank. Shut me eyes, I think, and slid down the plank. The matelot caught me at the bottom. He carried me down an alleyway and put me in a little cabin. He said, 'Now, stop there Tommy and I'll bring you a cup of tea.' Within about 5 minutes he came down with the biggest cup of tea I've ever seen in my life. It was fantastic. I had a couple of sips and I thought I was home. I went outside and I found some of my mates talking so we stood in a ring and passed this tea round until it was empty. Believe me, it was lovely to be on that ship. Then I went back into the little cabin and I lay on the floor. I got one of those old-fashioned lifebelts, folded it

Following spread: Exhausted troops on their return to England. *(IWM C1748)*

up and put it down. I slacked off my tunic, put my head down and slept, and I didn't wake up until we got to Folkestone harbour. They said we'd been bombed on the way over but I didn't know a thing about it.

When we got into Folkestone, the people were giving us cigarettes and chocolate and cake. They were fantastic. And every stop on the way to Bristol, when we got on the train, there was tables laid out and tea in jam jars, because they'd run out of crockery, giving it to the troops. They couldn't do enough. We got off just outside Bristol. There was a lady stood outside – I think she was about 40 – and she had a couple of little kiddies and she was throwing her arms round every bloke and thanking him for what he'd done. It was fantastic. I said to my mate, 'Anybody would think we'd won the bloody war.' They gave us cards to write on and you could send them to your parents or your wife. I posted two and neither of them got through.

My wife was working in the post office in Bibury at that time. She was a telephone operator and as the cards came in she used to jump on her bicycle, pedal off down the village and give them to the people so they didn't have to wait for the delivery in the afternoon. Then she suddenly realised that she hadn't

had one from me. She was very worried, she was very young. I managed to get out of Horfield barracks, where we were taken and to a telephone box and I rang her up to tell her I was back. It was wonderful. I had a mate, who was a civilian, and he lent me his car to come home to my wife. I pulled up outside the post office and she was there. It was very emotional. Well, she just come straight round and she put her arms round me. It was something you can't describe. It was like you'd got something back again: you'd lost it, but you got it back. At times I never thought I'd see her again.

Joe Trinder's wife, Iris. Their reunion was very emotional.

JIM LOFTUS

Orders came that we would vacate Cassel on the night of 29 May. A chappie called Eddie Farmer, who was the colour sergeant, killed a pig so we had something to eat. That was the last we had to eat for a long time. We left Cassel by first light, which was about four in the morning, and the order came to make for a wood. Their mortars chased us the length of the wood. Wherever we ended up, their mortars hit us. They knew where we were. The mortars were very effective; they would hit the trees and explode. But as soon as you heard the mortar, you were on the move. Then, while we were in the wood the order came to make for Dunkirk. My thoughts were, 'Where the bloody hell is Dunkirk?' I was a sergeant but I had no map, no compass, no binoculars, nothing. Anyhow, the general consensus was that it was up a long road.

I ended up with six people. We had no food, no water and no sleep. You were exhausted and you'd see a barn with hay, so you'd move into it, climb the ladder and sleep upstairs. Then the farmer would come and chase us out. We didn't know at the time but had the Germans found us there, the farmer and his wife and family would have been killed so I would have done exactly the same had it been the reverse. We moved on from there, chased out, literally chased out and we moved off down the road. All we wanted was to lay down somewhere and pinch something for food but we couldn't get anything. I was starving; everybody was starving. We did find a tin of Ideal milk, half full, and we started drinking that, had a sip each. But water was the main thing we couldn't get. The ditch water was no good to us. We had to dispose of our packs because if you were crawling along, they would see the top of them. We came to a ditch, got into it and decided we'd stay there, wait until dark and then move across the road. One chap didn't. He got up and he moved across the road. He didn't get to the middle before he was dead. The Germans had fixed guns so we crawled into the road, pulled him back and just marked the spot where he was killed.

We then moved on further and we came across a wood. I thought it was funny that there were sounds coming from it. We looked and there was a staff car of the German Army inside the entrance. Good God. Out came half a dozen people, took our rifles, smashed them against the trees, and you're prisoners of war. To be captured so young, at 20 years old, not knowing what the next step was going to be – I was frightened. I'd heard a lot of tales about the Germans, what they did to prisoners, and I was scared. It was so bad that for the first three years after coming home I had nightmares. That initial arrest, being taken from freedom, it's hard to explain. But that first group that held us, they looked after us. Most of them spoke English. The *Oberst* (Colonel) himself was a proper toff. His English was perfect. But the soldier element was all around this field and there must have been 2,000 of them. What chance did we have, fighting a couple of thousand Germans?

I wasn't sure what was going to happen so I put my battle bowler on the floor under the staff car and I slept, possibly for an hour. The soldier element was coming up to see what the prisoners were like and they gave us coffee. On top of this staff car was a plate of sandwiches and when I woke up the *Oberst* said, 'Eat those sandwiches between you.' That was the first thing we had to eat for seven days. Then the second line, the bully boys, came to pick us up. I was a cocky little sod. I had three stripes on my arm: they couldn't do anything to me. But they did. That's when we got a rifle put across our back and we were kicked. I know my battle bowler was taken off me by this big fella from the police of the German Army. He put one on me which must have been a size 15 and I took a size 7 hat. He pulled it straight down over my head and told me to walk down the street. He dared me to take it off. We felt humiliated. We went there to do a job and we didn't do it. We had no back up and we weren't fit. We weren't fit to fight. I was captured on 5 or 6 June 1940, released on 22 April 1945. Lots of young life gone, but at least you were alive.

LEN LLEWELLYN

When I got to the beach, I decided that I would stay and help as many get away as possible. I thought I could swim out to the boats any time I wanted to because I was a strong swimmer. I could swim for three hours non-stop in the sea. They were sending rowing boats from the small craft to the beach to collect us but they couldn't come right on to the beach so people had to wade out. The water was up to your chest and

Len Llewellyn risked his life to help his colleagues to escape.

men like Joe Trinder couldn't have done it. They wouldn't have been able to get in the boat if it hadn't been steadied because it was tossing about. So there was six of us and we decided to wade out to hold the boats steady, three each side of these rowing boats. We were helping the soldiers in to get them away.

But all the time we were on the beach we were getting machine-gunned and bombed. We didn't have anything on the beach to protect us – no slit trenches dug or anything like that. There were too many people on the beach for that. Every couple of hours you'd have about three or four Stukas machine-gunning the beach. The beach was crowded, so they were bound to hit someone. You were lucky if you weren't hit. At one time I had a bomb fall within about 2 yards of my head and it didn't explode. These bombs were falling and you could hear them coming down because they made a whining sound. Well, you could see them actually. Some further up the beach exploded. I just went down to the ground and, 'Thump,' just about 2 yards away from me the tail fins were poking out of the ground.

I was on the beach for about five days, getting the men away on these rowing boats. The boat that I eventually went in was just a fishing vessel. I was covered in diesel and that was the terrible thing. I know I was very sick because of the diesel fumes. I went down below deck and although I had very little inside of me, I was seasick. I had a khaki uniform and the crude oil was like tar and stuck to it. I was covered. I discarded my uniform and put on a ladies' wrap-around apron. That was all I had on when I landed. I must have looked a sorry sight because I hadn't shaved for about three weeks. I had a beard and was like a minstrel with all this black diesel over me. When I got back to Ledbury I had to have a stood-up bath in petrol. I thought there should have been a sign up saying 'No Smoking'.

But while I was loading the boats, no thoughts ever came in my head about getting killed. I was too lucky for that. I was content to stay there and help as many get in the boats as possible. I was 'Lucky Lew'. I was born under a lucky star.

THREE

FEAR NOTHING

501 Squadron and the Battle of Britain

During the Battle of France and the Battle of Britain, No.501 (County of Gloucester) Fighter Squadron proved itself as one of the most capable Hurricane squadrons of the war. Formed in Filton on 14 June 1929, 501 Squadron was one of Britain's first Special Reserve units, introduced following Lord Trenchard's plan for the creation of a Citizen Air Force and formed along Territorial lines as a back up to the RAF. Based around a small staff of regular airmen, 501's pilots were mainly volunteer part-timers and weekend-flyers, often those with a passion for flying, like Michael Smith and Keith Aldridge. Other recruits were encouraged to join the

Filton airfield readied for war, 1939. *(IWM HU83749)*

501 Squadron in France, May 1940. Michael Smith is standing far right.

squadron by their employers. Bill Green worked at the Bristol packaging company Mardon, Son & Hall and one of its managers, Montague Clube, also happened to be 501's Squadron Leader.

501 was mobilised for war on 23 August 1939 and at Filton airfield trenches were dug and tents erected in readiness for operations. In order to bring the squadron up to full fighting strength, highly trained NCO pilots like James 'Ginger' Lacey and Kenneth 'Hawkeye' Lee were drafted in from units around the country to supplement 501's part-timers and by November the squadron was flying patrols over the Bristol Channel. In December the squadron was moved from Filton to RAF Tangmere in Sussex and there they waited until on 10 May 1940, the Blitzkrieg began. Many of the original auxiliary pilots, like Keith Aldridge and Bill Green, were still undergoing training, but within hours the rest of the squadron, including Michael Smith, found themselves on the way to Betheniville in France where they were to form part of the Advanced Air Striking Force.

501 Squadron Hurricanes, recognisable from the registration SD, scramble from Hawkinge on 15 August 1940. Both of these planes were shot down just three days later. *(IWM HU3093)*

Disaster struck the next day: one of the two Bombay transport planes carrying the ground crews and reserve pilots crashed on landing and three members of 501 were killed, including much-respected Adjutant Flying Officer Percy. The squadron was soon in action against the Luftwaffe but was forced to withdraw towards the coast as German forces pushed through France. Following the evacuation of the BEF from Dunkirk, the pilots and ground crew of 501 returned to England and arrived back at Tangmere on 20 June. Figures vary but squadron records show that 501's pilots shot down forty-four German aircraft during the Battle of France and produced three ace pilots. The cost of this success was the loss of five pilots killed in action, among them Michael Smith who died after abandoning his Hurricane when it was hit by fire from a Messerschmitt 110 near Mézères.

Within a fortnight of returning to England, 501 Squadron was once again declared operational. With a new commanding officer, Squadron Leader Henry Hogan, it was transferred to Middle Wallop in Kent before being moved to Gravesend on 25 July as part of No.11 Group; its forward operating base was at Hawkinge. This was the start of 501's Battle of Britain and in the months that followed the squadron established itself as a formidable fighting force. Its pilots demonstrated many feats of skill and courage throughout the battle, perhaps none more incredible than that carried out by Kenneth 'Mac' McKenzie on 7 October. Flying over the English Channel he attacked a formation of Me109s. Having damaged one aircraft he flew in for the kill only to find himself out of ammunition but rather than turn for home, 'Mac' flew alongside the damaged Messerschmitt and brought his wing tip violently down on the enemy's tail plane, forcing it into the sea. For this act of determination, Kenneth McKenzie was awarded the Distinguished Flying Cross.

During the summer of 1940, 501 had thirty-five days of continuous engagement with the Luftwaffe, the highest number recorded by any Hurricane squadron. Its pilots shot down between ninety and 100 enemy aircraft. Ten of them could claim in excess of five kills and were thus awarded the title 'ace'. These statistics make 501 Squadron the second most successful Hurricane squadron of the Battle of Britain and the fifth highest scoring squadron overall. With eighteen kills to his name, 'Ginger' Lacey became one of Fighter Command's top-scoring pilots and was awarded the Distinguished Flying Medal plus Bar. Unfortunately, 501 Squadron could claim another record; the cost of success was the loss of forty-three planes, the highest number lost by any Hurricane squadron during that period. Again figures vary, but about twenty pilots were lost with those aircraft.

When they were called into action, both Keith Aldridge and Bill Green had had very limited experience flying Hurricanes and both had miraculous escapes, as they describe vividly in this chapter. With a life expectancy of somewhere in the region of 20 hours, it was a feat for the part-time flyers of 501 Squadron just to live up to the squadron motto – *Nil Time*, Fear Nothing.

BILL GREEN

I was born in 1917 in Bristol and went to St Gabriel's School where I stayed until I was 14. I left school at midday, looked in the evening paper to see what jobs were going and there was an advert for an errand boy in Cheltenham Road for a family called Hallett. I'd always been reasonably well blessed academically – I'd been head boy – and when I went they said, 'This is not a very good job, you know.' I said, 'I know, I just want a job.' So he gave me quarter of ham and sent me over to Stoke Bishop with it, which was no mean feat for a 14-year-old. I worked there for about six months and then my father, who worked in a cardboard box factory in Temple Street called E.H. Mogford, told me to give my

Bill Green.

notice in. He said that I was going to work with him. That's where I met Bertha, who became my wife. I just took one look into her beautiful brown eyes and I was gone. Anyway, that started my career in paper boxes and cartons, and eventually I left there and worked for Mardon, Son & Hall. To work for Mardon's before the war was like winning the pools and people's names were put down before they were conceived! They were really very supportive of all the Territorial military activities and made it convenient for their employees to join one or other of them. I joined 501 Squadron as an aero engine fitter under training, bottom of the pile.

Opposite: James 'Ginger' Lacey became one of the most successful and best known Battle of Britain pilots. *(IWM CH8459)*

Bill and Bertha married on 3 June 1940; the Battle of Britain began a month later.

I had no desire to fly planes. I didn't have ambitions of that sort. I was just happy being in the Auxiliary Air Force. We used to go at weekends and sometimes a Thursday evening. I became a leading aircraftsman fitter within about 18 months, which was quite monstrous, really, because I knew nothing about engines, but I was allocated an aeroplane together with a partner who was the rigger. He did everything outside of the engine and I did the engine. He was better educated than I and in late 1938 he said, 'I'm leaving the squadron, I'm going to learn to be a pilot.' I was green with envy, really, so I went to the CO and said that I wanted to do the same. It was sheer cheek on my part because I'm sure I wouldn't have had the educational qualifications, but he said, 'Wouldn't you rather stay with the squadron and fly?' I said, 'Yes, but that's only for commissioned people, not a lowly bod like me.' And he said, 'I'm telling you this in confidence: I'm getting an establishment for six non-commissioned pilots. Wouldn't you rather stay with us and become a sergeant pilot?' I thought I'd won the pools. At that time, the squadron was only for acting pilot officers, people who were well connected, usually with a very good education and often with money. In October 1939, after we were mobilised, they sent me off to an elementary flying training school at Hanworth. The thought of becoming a pilot was beyond my wildest dreams and it was wonderful for me. I couldn't believe my luck when it happened. I was the only one in the whole squadron who was elevated from being a tradesman to becoming a pilot under training.

Principally, my training was flying replacement aircraft to various airfields around Biggin Hill. One day in August I flew one across to Gravesend where my squadron was based. I ran into the CO and he asked me how I was getting on. I said, 'I've done about six hours, mostly ferrying aircraft.' He said, 'That's no good. You come back here. We'll train you a lot quicker than that.' I said, 'When

Bill Green.

do you want me back, sir?' He said,
'Tonight.' I skedaddled back to Biggin Hill,
collected my bits and pieces, and arrived
back at Gravesend at dusk if not dark. I was
shown a hut and was next to a chap called
Ginger Lacey, who became quite well known.
I was given a cup of cocoa and a hunk of
cheese and bread. I said, 'What time do they
have supper?' and was told, 'That's it.'

Then at about three in the morning, it
was dark and someone was shaking me and
shining a light in my face. I said, 'I'm
Green, I'm new.' He said, 'Yes, I know.
You're Green Three.' So I found myself out
of bed and dressed and walking down the
airfield to my aeroplane, carrying my
parachute. I said to Lacey, 'What's this
Green Three business?' He said, 'Well, we're
Green section. That's the last section. We're
at the rear of the squadron and instead of
flying in formation, we weave, just do turns
to the right and the left to make sure the
squadron doesn't get bounced from behind.' He said, 'When you see me do a
turn to the right, do a turn to the left.' When I saw him go, I did what I
thought was the shortest and the gentlest turn that had ever been done. When I
turned back, there was nobody there: the squadron was gone. When you
imagine, if you turn 90 degrees, and they're going 300 miles an hour plus one
way, and you're doing 300 miles an hour plus this way, it doesn't take long for
them to be out of sight.

During the Battle of Britain I think most people realised we were under
attack, that there was a likelihood of an invasion, and that we were part of the
overall plan to try and frustrate or prevent this invasion. We had a visit from
some senior brass hat from Divisional Headquarters who said that we were
expecting to be invaded, that the Germans would come in gliders towed by
Junkers 88s, and that we were to try and destroy the towing aircraft. He said

During the first phase of the Battle of Britain, the Luftwaffe targeted shipping in the English Channel. *(IWM PL8922)*

when we fired at the gliding aircraft with the troops in it, we weren't to be satisfied with seemingly damaging the glider. We were to fire until we saw blood coming out of the hinges of the frame of the door. That was really the measure of the expectancy of being invaded. In retrospect I would have appreciated it if someone, the CO perhaps, had got us together to say, 'Now then lads, I want you to understand the importance of the job you're doing and it all depends on you.' I would have valued that. I think it would have put a sharper edge on my appetite for what I had to do and taken the edge off the down side of it. And I would have also valued someone telling me how to fly the aeroplane effectively to avoid being shot out of the sky because I was totally green, as indeed were a number of others. The problem that the Air Force had was that the old sweats who had been through the Battle of France and had done quite a bit of flying pre-war were surviving, whereas we were not surviving, so they were carrying the weight. We were arriving, being shot down, hospitalised, and they were having to carry the weight and I think it was a heavy burden for them. I think they did a fantastic, fantastic job. But no one ever sat me down and said, 'This is how you do it, Bill.

If this happens, you do this,' or 'If that happens you do that, and you mustn't do that if you want to survive.'

It was all a strange new world to me. I knew little or nothing about what was going on and everybody was too involved looking after their own life to spend time with sprogs like me. There wasn't much chat during the day. I think people were too tired. They were either sleeping or resting. For me it was a very nervous period. You were in this dispersal tent and there was a field telephone there. Every time it rang it might be an order to scramble and that meant you were going to have to get into the air to face enemy aircraft, and possible death or wounding. I think they all dreaded the sound of that telephone. I really feared it and I hoped it would never ring!

I only flew in combat during the Battle of Britain for nine days, from 20 August to 29 August. But I crammed about twenty-six missions in those nine days, so that was about the scale of it. About three times a day you were scrambled for something or other. I felt more than vulnerable because of my inexperience, so I was more than Green by name and green by nature, and I wasn't alone in this. You knew how to fly the aeroplane, you knew how to do turns and you knew how to do aerobatics, sort of, in it. But I'd had no

Like many others Bill dreaded the ring of the telephone, which often meant it was time to scramble.

experience in firing my guns and you didn't really know that much about the deflection you had to use to attack an aeroplane. You certainly didn't know how to effectively do a parachute jump.

On 24 August we were vectored to Manston, which is near Margate. We were vectored on to some Ju88s which were diving to bomb Manston. We pulled in behind them and I was just closing in with my gun button on 'fire' when suddenly there was a big bang. The aeroplane rocked and my cockpit screen and the cockpit hood were covered with black oil. My engine stopped, then started and was spluttering. I knew that I'd been hit by something and I now know it was the ack-ack, firing at the 88s and hitting us, or me at least. So I managed to get it back to Hawkinge from the height we were at and crash landed it on Hawkinge airfield. At times like this you fear for your life. Everybody treasures their life. You know when you're hit it could be the end of your life, or you could be burned badly or whatever. And of course I was mindful of having Bertha at home.

During the Battle of Britain time off was unknown. You were just flying and flying and flying. But every now and again the Tannoy would go and it would say either A flight or B flight stand down. On one occasion I flew down to Whitchurch in Bristol, which was then Bristol Airport. At that time Bertha was living with her mother in Bedminster, so I just arrived. She had knitted me a new pair of socks. I wore them back when she saw me off the next day. When I got back to Gravesend the weather was bad and the cloud was quite low so I didn't think that there would be any bombers to attack or that we would be able to get off the ground to attack them. I sat down in the dispersal tent and wrote to Bertha, thanking her for the day we'd just had in Bristol and saying that I didn't want her to worry because the cloud was so low that day that we certainly wouldn't fly. Then at about 6 o'clock in the evening we were scrambled, much to my amazement. That was 29 August.

We went up and rendezvoused above about 12,000 feet of cloud. We were told to go to Red Queen, which was the code name for Deal. When we got to Deal we were told to orbit, and all the time you were orbiting you were mostly nervous about what might be behind you, especially when you orbited into the sun. We were told that we were to look out for 200 Me109s, 'snappers' they were called in code. I saw absolutely nothing but suddenly there was a crash of glass. The windscreen in the Hurricane was about 1¼ to 1½ inches thick, supposedly bullet-proof. What it was I don't know, but something crashed through there and made a hole larger than a tennis ball. I heard the glass falling around my feet and I immediately started to get covered, swamped, with liquid, which I presumed was glycol, the coolant in the engine. I realised the aeroplane was finished; the stick was just like nothing. I realised I had to get out. We were at 20,000 feet and I already had the hood back. I got as far as taking the weight off my bottom, on my feet, and had pulled the pin of the Sutton harness ready to get out when suddenly I was out, out in space.

I started to rotate, and I heard my flying boots go past my ears; my legs were obviously spread-eagled. I thought, 'My God, I'll never find my parachute.' As I was rotating, I was grabbing everywhere and I eventually found the ripcord and pulled it. I thought, 'Great, I'm safe, I'm okay.' Then suddenly I saw a piece of white something do two eccentric circles, just going away from me. This turned out to be the drogue parachute. This was the last thing that was packed and it had springs inside it. When you pulled the ripcord it was released and the springs opened like an umbrella. That then dragged the main canopy out of its pack and down you went. But in my case, the cords of the drogue parachute must have been severed, so when I pulled the ripcord it was free to open up and shot off into space. As a consequence, the main canopy just fell out of its pack and wrapped itself up between my legs and round me just like a shroud. And that's how I began to fall through space.

I remember thinking that this was it. I was wrapped up in the parachute and either I had to stop rolling forward and roll backwards – and I had no idea how

After being shot down on 29 August 1940 Bill worried about ruining the new socks which Bertha had knitted for him!

to do that – or the wind had to get under some part of the parachute, inflate it and kick me back. I was quite certain that I was going to die and I was searching for my end through my thoughts of Bertha. I remember thinking, 'I wonder if Bertha would wonder what my end was like.' I was continuing to try to push the parachute back, I thought forlornly, but the wind must have got under one of the folds and kicked the parachute open. It kicked me back and I realised I was okay. The quietude of that situation hits you more than any noise you could ever hear. When you're rushing through the air at 255 feet per second the noise is tremendous. You only have to stick your head out of a car window at 60 miles per hour to realise that. And then when it suddenly stopped and I was just hanging there, in absolute blissful safety as it were, it really hit me so much, that quietude. The whole thing was absolutely wonderful and I thought, 'I'm all right.' I looked around and there were electricity pylon cables level with me and the trees were above me on one side. I relaxed my legs and I was on the ground.

The whole thing took about a minute and a quarter I think. I remember sitting in this field with no boots and these new socks, looking at the cowpats and thistles, thinking, 'I've got to go walking thought this lot with these brand new socks on that Bertha's knitted me.' That was not bravado, because I was anything but brave. Then two chaps came running down the field with guns, thinking that maybe I was a German. I went to get up and realised I couldn't. They had to help me into the farmhouse and I realised then there was something wrong with my leg. It was cannon splinters in my knee. Then I was collected and taken back to Hawkinge where I was taken to the sick quarters and a doctor named Samuels ripped away my trousers. He had a long knitting needle and he poked it around in this hole in my leg, and whether it was the reaction or the pain, I passed out.

I went to see the CO the next day and I told him about my fall. He looked at me and he said, 'You mean to say you still want to fly?' And it started me thinking. In November 1940, I was posted to 504 Squadron at Filton. They had been posted there because Filton airfield had been bombed. Bertha was living with her mother in Weymouth Road in Bedminster and I got permission to live with her there because 504 were a day squadron and we stood down at dusk. We'd only been married in the June and it was the first time really that I'd lived at home with Bertha's parents. Only a few days after my fall I was in bed and I awoke to realise that I'd wet the bed. I'd never ever done such a thing and I was so embarrassed, being newly married, sleeping with my wife in my in-law's home. I'm sure that it was the reaction to the fall because I'd sat up in bed and shuddered. Then I realised that the bed was wet. For many, many years after

Bill Green's lucky escape was carefully recorded in his log book.

that, until relatively recently, I would have the same experience, excluding the bed wetting.

On 24 November I said to Bertha, 'I think I ought to call in and see mum and dad.' My parents lived in Easton, so as I was cycling home from Filton I called in and had some tea with them. The air-raid sirens had gone but the air-raid sirens were always going and nobody paid any attention because nothing ever happened. My little sister, Rita, came in and said, 'Dad, there's a lot of lights in the sky.' So I went out and I saw all these parachute flares, hundreds of them descending, lighting up the city. I said to my father, 'This is it dad, you'd better get in the shelter.' I got on my bike and started cycling like a maniac, trying to get to Bedminster before it started, forlornly as it turned out, because when I got to Old Market Street, down came the bombs in quantity. I dived into a surface air-raid shelter outside of a pawnbrokers on the corner of what is now Temple Way. I was in this surface shelter then from about 7 o'clock, till midnight. That's how long it lasted. It was absolutely horrifying. You could have stood in the doorway and read the newspaper by the light of the fires that were burning. After this bombing, I was patrolling over Bristol, because we patrolled Bristol constantly, and I counted fifteen fires still smouldering. That was about two days afterwards. I felt angry that my city had been so desecrated and that I had been unable to do anything about it.

Bill (centre) was transferred to an instructional role, which he was desperate to leave so that he could prove himself in combat.

I had thought that during the Battle of Britain my inexperience ill-equipped me for doing what I had to do, so that I was shot out of it before I'd had a chance to prove my capability to myself, or to anybody else that might be interested. I was then drafted to an instructional role, which most Battle of Britain people were, and getting out of the flying training command was like getting out of jail. But I wanted to get back to a combat squadron because I wanted to prove to myself that I could do it. I had to do it for my family, especially for my young son. I didn't want to leave this world with there being a doubt about my courage or my ability to fly in combat. I did a fair bit of lobbying and eventually got posted back to operations.

It was after the D-Day invasion, round about October 1944. I was flying a Tempest V, which was then our most modern fighter aeroplane, in 56 Squadron. Our main role really was patrolling over Germany, firing at anything that moved, especially if it was of a military nature – a train, a convoy of troops. We were strafing these things which were often heavily defended. We very rarely ran into enemy aircraft because they were very short of fuel and very short of aircraft. But on one occasion, on 2 February 1945, we had gone somewhere in north-west Germany, were engaged in combat and I zigged when I should have zagged and I was hit. This time my parachute worked and I landed in a wood where I was taken prisoner by a German farmer within seconds. Thus began

Flying Officer Bill Green in 1943.

three months of fascinating experience, with Germany collapsing. I arrived home on 8 May, VE day, and when I got to Weymouth Road, the street was full of trestle tables with kids having jelly and sausage rolls. When I got out of the cab, they all stood up and started cheering and I was so embarrassed.

I was no hero. I know now that I wasn't a hero. I was just like most of the other people who realised the value of their life and how much they cherished it and how much they had to live for, especially those of us who were married. I feel very privileged to have been one of those people who happened to be there at that time. You'd been trained as a pilot, or half trained in my case, and you had to do the best you could under the given circumstances. I'm proud now that I did it; I'm glad I did it.

KEITH ALDRIDGE

After I left school the aircraft industry interested me, so I went in with the Bristol Aeroplane Company, on the engine side. That was on the airfield at Filton and right in the corner of the airfield was 501, the City of Bristol Squadron, who were flying Gauntlets at that time. They were visible from the engine test sheds and I had a sneaking feeling right from the word go that I'd like to join that élite band out in the corner there. And as it turned out I was accepted: you were privileged to be a member of 501 Squadron. It was a flying club, if you like, and I was interested to see if I could learn to fly. It was entirely at weekends. The pilots were weekend flyers but the ground crew were permanent RAF people. If you were going to join them, you were sort of on probation as an acting pilot officer, and although I was with them for eighteen months, I didn't feel I was a member of the squadron because I hadn't obtained

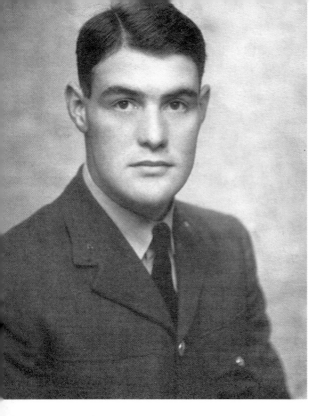

Acting Pilot Officer Keith Aldridge at the age of 19.

my wings. When they went on a wartime basis, I still wasn't trained within the squadron. I was still very much a sprog pilot.

I was shifted off to different training schools after war broke out – to Hanworth airfield (I think flying Magisters) and back to South Cerney, flying Hawker Hinds, Audax, Harts, biplanes. You know, old vintage bombers. So I learned how to fly but not how to fight. I hadn't any fighting instinct in me as such. I was merely a weekend flyer who learned to fly. They graded me as exceptional but that really didn't mean very much. I think all pilots were graded exceptional because if they weren't, they weren't accepted. My first job was finding accommodation for the call-up people who were coming from the reserves, which in those days meant finding sufficient straw and hay to put down in the hangars for people to spend the night on. I didn't realise I would have to fight. When I first had to fly in combat, I hadn't even had three hours flying in a Hurricane, which was the aircraft one was supposed to be operational on. It was all right. I could fly it but not aggressively. Unless you can fly automatically and aggressively you aren't going to go very far, and I didn't.

I didn't make any close friends and relationships during the war. The time we were with our co-pilots was short and I didn't talk to them particularly. They weren't friends. They didn't have anything to offer me and I had nothing to give them. Nothing was passed on. You'd have thought the old pilots would have said, 'Look, this is the form. Come up and dogfight with me,' or whatever. That was never offered and never taken. If I had had just a little experience of dogfighting with another person, watching how his controls moved in front of me and anticipating what he was going to do, that would have been an experience which would have made me a better pilot. Perhaps a much better fighter pilot. I would like to think that I was a good pilot but I hadn't the bulldog spirit, whatever you like to call it. No, I hadn't got that.

501 pilots act out a mock scramble in August 1940. Their smiles reveal that this is not the real thing. *(IWM HU 57452)*

The first time I flew in combat, the alarms went – the Germans were bombing the airfields around. There were three squadrons on the airfield and they'd all taken off. There were a couple of spare Hurricanes left around with no pilots for them. I think it was the Station Commander said, 'Are you a pilot? Well, take this one off. Get it off the ground.' So I took it off the ground. I didn't know where I was going but I thought, 'Well, I'll hang around somewhere near the airfield and if they're gonna bomb it I might see them and have a squirt at them.' But I hadn't a clue what was going on. The radio was cackling away with the usual chatter which comes through, and I eventually met up with a Messerschmitt 110, I think. I got up on his tail and was about to fire at him and he suddenly did a turn. I wasn't ready for him doing a turn, so he must have been laughing his head off. Of course any decent pilot would have turned with him and given him a nasty fright. But I was so slow and so inexperienced I just didn't.

If you're brought to readiness, you sit around with your Mae West on, all the kit's ready, and then a phone call comes through and that means everybody sort of jumps out of their chairs. Then the order comes, 'Scramble,' and you dash into your aircraft. Your aircrew help strap you into the cockpit and make sure that everything's right. The idea was to be able to get the squadron off within a couple of minutes. If you were a bit lazy and you were 30 seconds late, then you had a lot of catching up to do to catch up with the squadron. I found that there really wasn't very much time to do cockpit checks if I wanted to get off with the squadron because they were experienced, they knew what was required and it was up to you to keep up with them. The flight commander said, 'Stick to my tail. You'll be all right.' I think the thoughts behind that were, if I stuck behind him I should get shot first before he got shot down, at least that was my attitude towards it. I didn't feel resentful of that. You didn't know any better. But I very quickly appreciated that if you were keeping your eyes on your number one, you had very little chance of seeing what was happening outside.

I don't think fear comes into it. You're flying and you know if you aren't careful somebody else is going to fire at you, so you're spending quite a lot of time looking around, seeing who's trying to get on your tail and shoot you down. Eighty per cent of my time flying on operations was spent looking behind me, seeing what was coming up behind, rather than what was in front. I don't know whether I was anything other than normal. Everyone was more worried about what was coming up behind. Anticipation was probably the worst part of it, you know: 'Where are they, I can't see them?' And what you can't see you get frightened about. When you see them, yes, then you can get terrified, but the adrenaline's building up so rapidly that you haven't got time to worry about your inefficiencies and your inexperience. You're there and make the best of it.

The Hurricane was a very sturdy aircraft. They said it was a good gun platform, because it had eight – eventually twelve – Browning 303 guns, and when you fire your guns, then you smell the cordite. Even though they're in the wings and far out from you, you can smell the guns and you can hear the rattle of them because you're putting out 1,300 rounds a minute from each gun – times eight, that's a lot of bangs going off. It was a manoeuvrable aircraft and you could certainly turn inside a Messerschmitt 109 at low altitude, not at high altitude. It wasn't any good at high altitude. Fifteen-thousand feet was about the maximum. The time you did get frightened was when you were in a dogfight situation. You think, 'Can I out-turn him?' And in this situation, every pilot in a fighter pilot has to fly the plane to its limit. In a dogfight you'd start pulling tighter and tighter turns and the time comes when either he knows that you're catching him closer or you know that he's turning inside you. Then one has various means of avoiding the situation, doing something rapid and

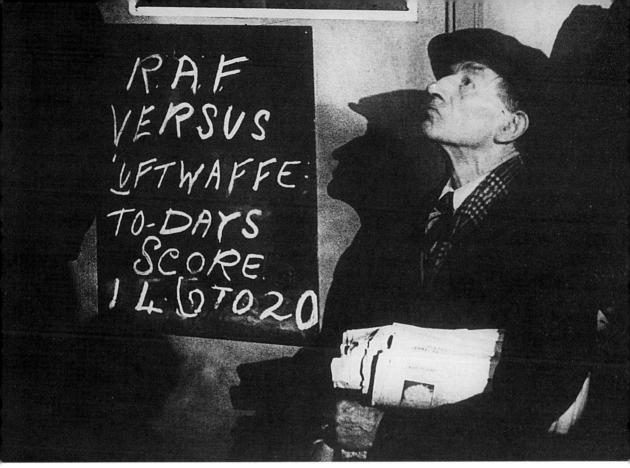

Although the pilots claim not to have been aware of the importance of their role, the daily dogfights became a source of fascination for the general public. *(IWM HU810)*

unexpected. Usually you'd do a reversal with a lot of rudder so that you skidded through the air. It doesn't matter what or where or why or how. If you do it rapidly enough, he can't follow you, unless he's very wide awake. And some of the Germans were wide awake. They could see the twitch of your control, and they'd be with you.

I don't think we realised the importance of the Battle of Britain. I appreciated that hell was being bombed out of London, and I thought, 'Thank God I'm not there.' It was a time of intense pressure undoubtedly, but I don't think I was unduly worried about the situation. I was terrified, yes, but I think everybody was terrified. I suppose I flew forty or fifty sorties in total. I don't think it was more than that. There was only four or five times when I used my guns, only four or five times out of fifty flights, and what damage I did I don't know. But it was very easy to lose contact. One minute the sky was full of aircraft and the next minute you couldn't see anybody. Extraordinary. And that's when you really start rubber-necking round, trying to see where everybody's gone.

One event is clear in my mind. The squadron was in a head-on situation and any head-on situation was alarming. I'm with eleven other pilots in fairly close formation and I'm not looking at my number one, or at whatever else the squadron is doing. I'm really focussing on the horde of bombers which is coming straight at us. It was the biggest formation of bombers I'd ever seen. I know I hadn't turned my gun sight on and I hadn't turned the safety catch on my guns into the firing position. This I'm starting to do as I'm making a closing situation. I'm doing 200mph and they're doing 170, and so the closing speed is very fast. You haven't got time to be frightened. Then I've got my finger on the button and it's firing and these bombers are coming past in a flash. The whole operation is only three, four, five seconds at the utmost I suppose. Five seconds of firing and you're through, and I think I probably closed my eyes the whole time through. And when I come out the other side, I can't see anybody. I can't see any aircraft, none of my own aircraft, none of the enemy aircraft, they've all gone, because I've gone straight through. I was just pleased to be out the other side and breathing.

I turn round and in the distance I can see the bombers disappearing. So I start chasing again, and there's ack-ack stuff coming up behind the bombers, and you can see there's some damage been done somewhere along the line. At that stage I was jumped by an Me109 or whatever and put on fire. When you're put on fire your brain doesn't work very well. There are things one can do to get out of an aircraft safely. They had told me that the best way to do it was firstly to ensure that your harness was undone and your canopy was open, then to turn the aircraft on its back and you drop out. Conversely, you can put your foot on the control column, push it hard forward and you come out like a champagne cork out of a bottle. Neither of which I did, because when you've got flames coming up from your feet, through up over your face, you aren't thinking very clearly. At least I wasn't. I'd forgotten to undo my straps and I remember a strap coming up and hitting the side of my face. I had burns on my legs and hands and face, mostly on the hands because I wasn't wearing gloves – I don't think 90 per cent of the pilots did. I had an oxygen mask on, which in point of fact is not a good thing to have on if there is a fire around because oxygen and fire is a good mixture for a good combustion. So I was interested in getting out no matter. I peeled out over the edge and, as anybody could have told you, you hit the tail plane on the way out. If you're lucky you only break your arm and shoulder, which happened to me. If it had been just a little bit higher it would have been my head and I wouldn't be here today.

There was no pain. Fright, yes, but adrenalin washes out all pain. I wasn't conscious of my shoulder and arm being shattered, not a bit of it. And then I was freefalling. I was at about 15,000 feet, I suppose, when I was hit. Now I get in my mind that I've got to pull the parachute cord with my right hand because the D handle which you pull was on the left side. As my right shoulder is completely non-functional, I make all the movements with my right hand to go over to the left-hand side, but it doesn't go. I'm still determined to pull it with my right hand, so I take it with my left hand and pull it across to my left-hand side, and then pull the cord. I'm waiting for the canopy to open and it does, with a bang. I was descending at about 120, 130mph, which is freefall speed, and suddenly the parachute pulled me up to 5mph in no time flat. That's all right if you've got your parachute on properly, because the parachute has straps which go between your legs and over your shoulders, and if it's nice and tight and snug, no problem. But if it's not tight and snug, as mine wasn't, well one of the straps comes over my testicles and I perforated one of my testicles. There was no pain, but in retrospect I must have screamed. No pain: the adrenaline was running so fast. There I am hanging down on the parachute, thinking, thank goodness all that's over. Then I look down at the fields of Kent and I can see the farmers and cyclists all chasing across the field with their pitchforks and the rest of it, coming to take the enemy.

I come down with a heck of a thump in a ditch and then around the corner comes an ARP man, revolver in hand, shaking like mad. I gave him a mouthful of my choicest English and he said, 'You can't be a German if you have such command of English. Must be English.' So there was no problem. There were a lot of people coming up, looking around, one of which was an old boy on a bicycle. He looks at me, turns round and dashes off on his bicycle. I thought, 'I dunno, no bleeding heroes around here, I've lost my fans straight away.' By this time the ambulance came and was getting ready to cart me off. But in between whiles, the old man on his bicycle comes charging down this little lane, coat tales flying, hurls his bike into the ditch, comes up to me with a glass and a bottle and says in an Irish accent, 'Would you care for a drop of brandy, sir?' Bless him, that was a nice touch. Inside no time at all I was in hospital being treated. The hospital was full of Air Force wounded, German and English. And they treated me for burns and splinted me up on a big body cast with my elbows all stuck out. That was my Battle of Britain.

It's hard to say what makes up a fighter pilot. There were a lot of heroic people in the Battle of Britain but I wasn't one of them, no way. Some of them were incredibly . . . brave is a stupid word. No, they were intent on completing a mission and downing the enemy, no matter. That needs a lot of courage and I didn't have it, I don't think. Not on purpose, that's for certain. I didn't consider myself the right type of mentality to get on to another aircraft and hang on to him come what may until I'd shot him down. But you had a responsibility to fire your guns in anger, did you not? You weren't up there to enjoy the air. And what's the alternative, conscientious objector? No, I'm not a conscientious objector, but I dislike killing people. I hadn't got that killer instinct, or whatever you like to call it. That wasn't part of my make-up. I think I had qualms about killing people. And the times that I have killed, and known I've killed, they are times which come back to haunt you, and you're never the same man again. That's war, I suppose, but it doesn't make it any nicer. Not for me anyway.

MARY LALONDE

I met Michael (Smith) at a hunt ball in Brockley Coombe in early 1939. We obviously were attracted because after that he rang me and we went out, and so

it grew. He was full of fun. Typical of what you might think a fighter pilot might be, and certainly there was a great glamour attached to the squadron, all of them. We were engaged in the late spring, early summer of 1939 and because the war was imminent we got married probably sooner than we would have done ordinarily, but we pushed it forward. Obviously he knew the dangers much more than I. You see, I was only 21 when we were engaged, and I must admit the thought of war, awful to say it now, but it was a little bit on the glamorous side. There was a sort of frisson of excitement about it all. But he knew the dangers much more than I of course, it never occurred to me.

He was at Filton for some time and I think they went to Tangmere in about October, after we were married in

Michael Smith and Mary were married on 30 September 1939.

Michael Smith (left) at Filton. On his right is Flying Officer Derek Pickup, who claimed the squadron's first enemy aircraft shortly after arriving in France.

September. There was no accommodation, of course, for wives at that time. I went down before Christmas, about November I suppose, and we had digs in Chichester when he was off duty. It was very difficult being apart because we were both very young. He was only 27 and I was 21, so it was tough. I used to go down sometimes for 48 hours until I eventually went down and lived in Chichester. And I was still working as a physiotherapist. We did write to each other, of course. We used to watch the postman come, he there and I here. I can't think it was daily, because of course they were on duty, and they were night flying and all the rest of it. But it was certainly three or four letters a week we used to write to each other. We were very newly married, you see, so we were telling each other how much we missed each other, and how much we loved each other, and how long it would be before we saw each other, all that sort of thing, as newly-weds would. I wasn't worried about Michael. It never occurred to me somehow that anything would happen. It shows how naïve I was at that age. Funnily enough, Michael was on 24 hours' leave and the phone went and he said, 'I bet that's the mess,' and it was. That was 11 May 1940 and they flew out to France that afternoon.

I came back to Temple Cloud that afternoon with his flight commander's wife and we rather threw things in our cars, so I had some of her things and she had

Above: Michael Smith (left) in France, shortly before he was killed.

Below: Michael Smith (right) with other members of the squadron including Ginger Lacey, who is in the centre background wearing the tin helmet.

some of mine. On the Monday I went over to see her to sort the things out and it was whilst I was away that the telegram came. In those days, we had a little postmistress, it was a little small village, and we had a little postmistress who always knew exactly what was in anybody's telegram. She used to come up and say to my mother, 'I'm very sorry that your aunt is ill,' as she handed her the telegram. But this particular time she came up in tears. That was middle of the day on the Monday, and I didn't get back home to my parents' house until about five. It's a funny thing, because I'm not in any way psychic, but as I drove up the drive my father had opened the garage doors, which was a thing he never did for me. I always had to open them myself. I wondered, I had a sort of funny feeling that things weren't quite as they should be. And of course when I went in, he told me that Michael had been killed.

It was an enormous shock, in fact such a shock that I lost my voice, I couldn't speak at all. I was in a sort of trance, I suppose, because it was such a shock. We'd been married such a short time. Seven months. My father had the telegram, but beyond that no information, just the telegram from the King. I did, of course, burst into tears, and I remember saying, 'No, no, it can't be.' After that I went really into deep shock. I remember the doctor being sent for and I was given some form of tranquilliser. My brother-in-law came to see me and it was difficult because I couldn't speak to him. But people were very kind. They were almost as shocked as I was because it was, of course, so early – nobody had really heard of any casualties. I remember it was a lovely summer. My father had a summerhouse in the garden and I think I spent a lot of my time there.

I think I was numbed for a long time. But I was very fortunate, being a physiotherapist, because one of the surgeons in Bristol, who had been a lecturer to me, called into the rectory. His name was Mr Priddy; he was well known in Bristol. He had heard what had happened, so he came to see my parents and he told them that he would like me to go to the Infirmary to learn plaster work, and then he wanted me to go to Winford, which was the EMS (Emergency Medical Services) orthopaedic hospital for the troops. That really saved my life in a way. I was on the point of volunteering for the WRAFs (Women's Royal Air Force), but I think I was more fulfilled in what I did during the war at Winford, dealing with the troops. Really and truly that was a miracle for me, and I remained at Winford until 1945.

The memory was always there, will be always there. It lessens. The old adage that time heals is true. I was busy and I was with other people, which helped. But I was lonely. The letters I had from Michael I kept, of course, and have still got them. They meant a tremendous amount to me, but I had all those letters

Above: The Hurricane Michael Smith was flying when he was killed, labelled SDM, is seen at the rear of this photograph taken at Filton. Several years ago, members of the Hurricane Society began a search for the plane in France.

Below: The recovery team finding Michael Smith's Hurricane.

Above: Mary Lalonde with part of the steering column of Michael Smith's Hurricane.

Below: The letter Michael Smith left for Mary. The envelope reads, 'Iron rations. Only to be taken in an extremely low condition, in other words never to be taken at all.'

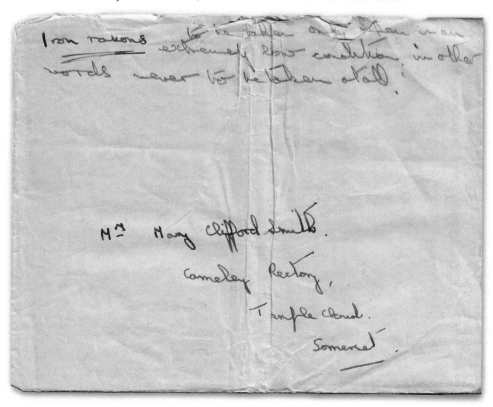

Michael Smith: he gave his life for peace for evermore.

before he was killed. Except the last one, which he gave to my father, which he called an 'iron ration'. He says in it that this is to be read if I was very low, or very depressed – 'Hopefully you will never have to read it.' Obviously he knew that this was the letter to be given to me if anything happened to him. It is a very poignant letter and a very loving letter, and a letter that made it quite clear that he hoped I would never have to read it. It was written within a fortnight of our marriage, extraordinarily enough, even though it wasn't given to my father until seven months later. It was the sort of letter that two youngsters would write to each other, deeply in love. I'd never read that letter again until recently. When I reread it I didn't cry, not after sixty-four years, but I was sad. It did sadden me. And I've had a very happy life since. But it's something that was an episode in my life that will never be forgotten, and in fact it was something that I was really very proud of. I was very proud of him. He gave his life for the country, for me, and he thought, I'm sure, for peace for evermore.

FOUR

FOR THOSE IN PERIL

The Men of the Royal and Merchant Navies

On the day war broke out, the German U-boat U-30 fired two torpedoes at what she thought was a merchant cruiser leaving Britain for America. But it was a dreadful mistake, and at approximately 7.40pm on 3 September 1939 the passenger liner *Athenia* became the first victim of the Battle of the Atlantic. Miraculously, most of her 13,581 passengers were able to board lifeboats; however, 118 people lost their lives. Mistake or not, the swift and devastating effect of this action made it quite clear that the U-boat would be a considerable threat to Britain's ability to defeat Germany. As an island power, Britain's survival rested on her ability to import food, oil and raw materials without which she could simply be starved into submission. Indeed Winston Churchill famously

The U-boat was the only thing Churchill feared during the war. *(HU40239)*

claimed that the U-boat was the only thing that frightened him during the war.

In 1939, Britain's merchant fleet was the largest in the world, numbering some 3,000 ships. But if this fleet were to survive the U-boat menace, it would need the full support of the Royal Navy and the reintroduction of the convoy system which had been implemented in the First World War. However, the Royal Navy was not the force it had once been and reliance upon old ships and tactics, in particular a belief in the strategic importance of the battleship, had left its vessels vulnerable to attack. Heavy losses at Dunkirk meant that there was a limited number of destroyers available for convoy duty and initially merchant vessels were only offered protection close to British shores. Furthermore, the fall of France left the Channel ports in enemy hands and the Atlantic was now within easy reach of the German fleet.

As a result, between June and September 1940 U-boats claimed 274 ships for the loss of only two of their own vessels. By early 1941 this figure had risen to a shocking 400 ships sunk. No wonder U-boat commanders

As well as the U-boats, giant German battleships like the *Bismarck, Tirpitz* and *Scharnhorst* (seen here) proved a formidable challenge to the Royal Navy, and an ever present threat to the merchant fleet. (IWM HU1042)

A corvette drops her depth charges in the hunt for a U-boat. *(IWM A22031)*

referred to this period as their 'happy time'. Much of this success came from the implementation of the 'wolf pack' system, introduced by commander of the German submarine fleet Admiral Doenitz, in which groups of U-boats, rather than solitary vessels, attacked Allied convoys.

Despite the dangers, merchant sailors like Maurice Ryan were proud to do their bit for Britain. Having experienced the terror of a sinking in the Atlantic, Maurice couldn't wait to get back to sea, despite doctor's advice and the best efforts of his parents. Many merchant sailors, however, had no option but to return to work as quickly as possible because, until 1941, a man's pay was stopped as soon as his ship was sunk, even if he had to endure many days at sea before being rescued. The risks were not, of course, limited to the Atlantic. Despite dreadful weather and violent seas, many convoys made the arduous journey to the Russian ports of Archangel and Murmansk. These Arctic convoys were able to deliver essential supplies to Russia, including 7,000 aircraft and 5,000 tanks, thereby maintaining the war on the Eastern Front. Others sailed the treacherous waters through the Straits of Gibraltar to Malta. These vitally important convoys had an undoubted influence upon Britain's success in North Africa as control of the Mediterranean prevented supplies reaching Rommel from Italy. Sailing close to shore, these convoys faced the additional threat of aerial attack and John Salinas had an eventful time as a gunner on the merchant ship SS *Troilus*, an experience he recalls with great enthusiasm.

The turning point in Britain's naval campaign came in December 1941 when the United States entered the war. American-built 'Liberty' cargo ships were produced quickly and efficiently to replace lost merchant vessels and long-range Liberator bombers began to track down and sink U-boats. British convoys also began to have more successes against the U-boats and ASDIC sonar technology assisted the small corvettes which attacked the enemy with explosive depth charges, as Cyril Stephens remembers.

By the end of 1943 the Battle of the Atlantic was virtually at an end and Admiral Doenitz's U-boats had finally been defeated. It had been the longest battle of the conflict and cost the lives of over 50,000 merchant sailors. But their sacrifice had kept Britain in the war and with control of the oceans restored to the Allies, the scene was set for the invasion of France.

MAURICE RYAN

I was good at geography at school and I thought to myself, 'I wanna get out and see some of that world.' What I really wanted to do, and I used to tell my

Maurice Ryan was desperate to go to sea and travel the world.

mother this, was to go to any country I came to, jump ship and live with the people, live their way of life.

I left school in 1938 and started a job as a mechanic, but I had to do all the odd jobs for a year before I could start my apprenticeship, so I said, 'No, I wanna go to sea.' Anyway, I was in the labour exchange one day and there was a big picture of what I thought was a pirate, this bloke with a woollen hat on and a tassel and a jersey, and I looked at that. This chap behind the counter said, 'Next.' I said, 'That's what I wanna be, like a pirate.' And he said, 'A seaman?' He said, 'I happen to be an ex-purser with the P&O line.' He told me what I needed to do, so I joined a training ship and from there on the banana boats, fishing boats, passengers boats, cruise liners and all that.

It was great to go to sea. I liked not seeing anything, just all that vast amount of water. It was so quiet and peaceful. You knew you were travelling to another world. You had something to look forward to. And not only that, the scenery was changing every day, different weather, and when you came into port and see all these colours – ships painted different colours – it was great. We weren't fearful or anything like that. My brother was in submarines, so I knew what to expect. We knew that if we didn't do our job, England would be beat and we would be under German rule. You'd see ships coming in and unloading from different parts of the world, with different cargoes, and we used to sing a song which went, 'We joined the Merchant Navy. We're gonna bring food into our country . . .' So to hell with the Germans. We knew the country had to have food and we were over the moon: we were so proud to be keeping the country afloat. We were proud to be a part of that.

In 1940, I sailed on the *Empire Merchant*, a banana boat from Avonmouth. I was only 16 and my job was Steward's Boy. I had to be up early, about half past four, and get tea on the bridge to the skipper or the mate, then down to the engine room to the duty engineers. I used to look after the dry stores, the tea and sugar. It wasn't kept on the deck, it was all raised up off the ground. I used to go round with a pan and shovel and you generally got rats' droppings, not many, but a few. So I'm sweeping up all the way round and who comes down but the chief steward, and he's got his dickie bow and all that lot on. He says, 'Come on then, boy, what's the matter. It's taking you long enough, innit?' I said, 'Yeah, but just a minute, sir, there's no rats' droppings.' With that he gave me a back hander. He said, 'Are you trying to tell me the ship's gonna sink?' Course I knew nothing of the saying that rats will leave a sinking ship.

On our second day out I was up early serving the tea and then all of a sudden, at twenty-five past six, there was such an explosion and the boat seemed to

The life-line is firm
thanks to the
MERCHANT NAVY

The role of the Merchant Navy is often overlooked, but during the Second World War some 50,000 merchant seamen lost their lives in enemy action. *(National Archives/PRO INF 13/213/52)*

Sixteen-year-old Maurice Ryan wasn't aware of the many superstitions followed by sailors.

jump out the water. The next thing the skipper shouts out, 'Make to the boats, we need to abandon ship', and as he's saying this we got another bang. That seemed to lift the ship a good way out the water and a few people got injured. The ship lurched to the starboard and she was filling up with water. I couldn't swim. It seemed a lifetime of events was happening in such a short space of time. I thought to myself, 'What do I do?' And I'm up on the boat deck and round the wireless house were all these sandbags. I was holding on to the rail and there were three lifeboats in the water then. I could see them and they were drawing away from the ship because they had to get away from the suction. I was really scared. I looked around and all I could see was water.

The skipper was still on the bridge, with another officer, and they're saying to me, 'Jump, jump, you bastard. Jump.' I let go of the rail for just a second and all of a sudden this sandbag burst and I slipped on the sand. Me feet shot from under me, I shot into the water and I went under. It's funny, you can open your eyes under the water and you see thousands, millions of bubbles. I came up and then I went under again. I didn't know which way to look. There was flotsam and jetsam and then the oil starts to get to you, up your nostrils and in your eyes. I saw my life coming back to me and I thought I'd had it. Anyway, I came up and all these hands grabbed me and pulled me into a lifeboat. I thought they'd broke me ribs or something, the way they grabbed me and pulled me in.

The ship was your home. You'd stick photos and postcards on the walls, and as you look at it as it's sinking, it's terrible. That's your home gone and all your personal possessions. While it's above water you think there's some chance, but all of a sudden you see it tip up and down she goes. Everybody looks. It's a terrible thing to see. Anyway, when we all got together after the ship had gone down the Captain said, 'The U-boat will be around here somewhere. So we'll keep together and tonight we'll shine a light on the sail and someone will see us.' I was the youngest on the boat and the chief steward gave me a kick and hid me under the thwart. He says, 'Stay under there, you bugger. If the U-boat surfaces, they'll take you back to Germany for propaganda purposes and they'll display you everywhere, just to show that they're so hard up in England they're sending boys like this to sea.' But the next morning the lifeboats were all separated and we were on our own. Then we had a seaplane come over. He circled and was Morse-coding with his lamp and he was gonna attempt to land. It was a bit choppy and as he came in to land we saw his starboard float break. He had to take off again, so he signalled that he would send assistance. Plenty of planes came over, but they can't see you. You're just like a pinhead in the water.

In them days, water and biscuits were kept in wooden barrels and a lot of this stuff fell out when the ship went down, so because we didn't know how long we were going to be in the lifeboat, the water was rationed and we only had one biscuit in the morning and one at night. It was August, but it's still chilly at sea. I was wet through and being a boy, I must have only been about 6 stone or something like that. You were in a cramped position and sometimes you got pains in your legs because you're not moving and your gear is clinging to you and your bones start to ache. You wonder, 'Are we gonna get over this? Are we ever gonna get ashore again?' Because you can't see anything around anywhere, just water. You all look at one another and everyone's got oil on their eyelashes and round their nostrils. Half of their gear was in rags and it was a terrible sight really. A sight I wouldn't wish to see again. But then you think, 'Here we are together, and we're alive.' We were just looking forward to getting rescued and getting back to sea again. We had coloured gangs aboard our ship because going down to Jamaica you had to take some of the locals. We had a coloured bosun. He was a big bloke and he was looking all the time and he kept saying, 'Land right ahead, Captain.' He was saying this every 5 minutes, but there was no land.

Everybody turns to prayer, especially seamen. It's funny, they're rough as so and so when they're on shore, drinking and what not. But anything like that, they all turned to prayer. You saw them, wet, bedraggled, cold, their heads bowed and you heard them say, 'Please God, get me out of this. Get me ashore, and I'll come back to sea again.' That was a comforting thing to me because in my younger days I was a choir boy, so I thought it was good to see men, monsters of men with real rough hands, praying to God. I prayed many times, consciously and unconsciously.

Altogether, we were at sea in the lifeboat for six days. Because I was the youngest, I got a lot of respect. But on the third day I don't know what happened but I fainted or something, I went unconscious. So I must have been very, very weak. It just shows you, I was in a terrible condition really, maybe near death. Maybe they thought I had died. Next thing, though, I'm on this rescue tug, the *Sylvania*. I woke up on the *Sylvania*. I don't know how I got aboard. I was manhandled of course. But we'd been picked up right up by Scotland. When we got torpedoed, we were right down the bottom of England and when we got rescued we were taken in to Greenock. So we'd gone right up the Irish Channel, but nobody could see us in the water because we were so small, like a pinhead.

When we got to Greenock, they took us to a big warehouse. Then they gave us clothing, a suit or whatever you want – jerseys, boots, shoes anything like that. The next thing, we had to go to London, escorted down to London. Course we had all these photographers and they were trying to grab me because I was such a boy. They were saying, 'Tell me the story, son. Come here, I'll give you a fiver, tell me the story.' Well £5 was a lot of money in them days. I only had £4 a month for going to sea. But I didn't take it, we didn't dare because we were being watched, the senior hands were watching. But once your ship gets sunk your money's gone, it stops immediately. In the Merchant Navy, your pay is stopped then and there. You don't realise this at the time, but we had to go to London to get paid off and I got £1 2s and 3d or something for going through all that. I reckon that's terrible, especially with us spending all that time in the lifeboat and suffering all that much and you don't get nothing for it.

We were sent home then, for about a month. When I got home, my mum cried. She'd had a premonition. At twenty-five past six in the morning, when we'd got torpedoed, her arm flew out when she was having a dream. My father woke up and she said, 'I've seen Maurice is in trouble. He's in the water.' But he told her to turn the light off and go back to sleep. The shock of what happened never showed on me, but after about a month my stomach started to vibrate. My mother got the doctor and the doctor said it was delayed shock. He told my mother that I had to stay ashore for about six months, but my stomach calmed down after a few weeks, so I told my mum I was going back to sea. She must have told my dad and he hid my discharge book, because you needed your discharge book to go to sea. When my mother and father were out at the pictures one day I looked upstairs in their bedroom, pulled the top drawer open and sure enough at the back was my discharge book. So shortly after that I went back to sea and I sailed in the convoys then.

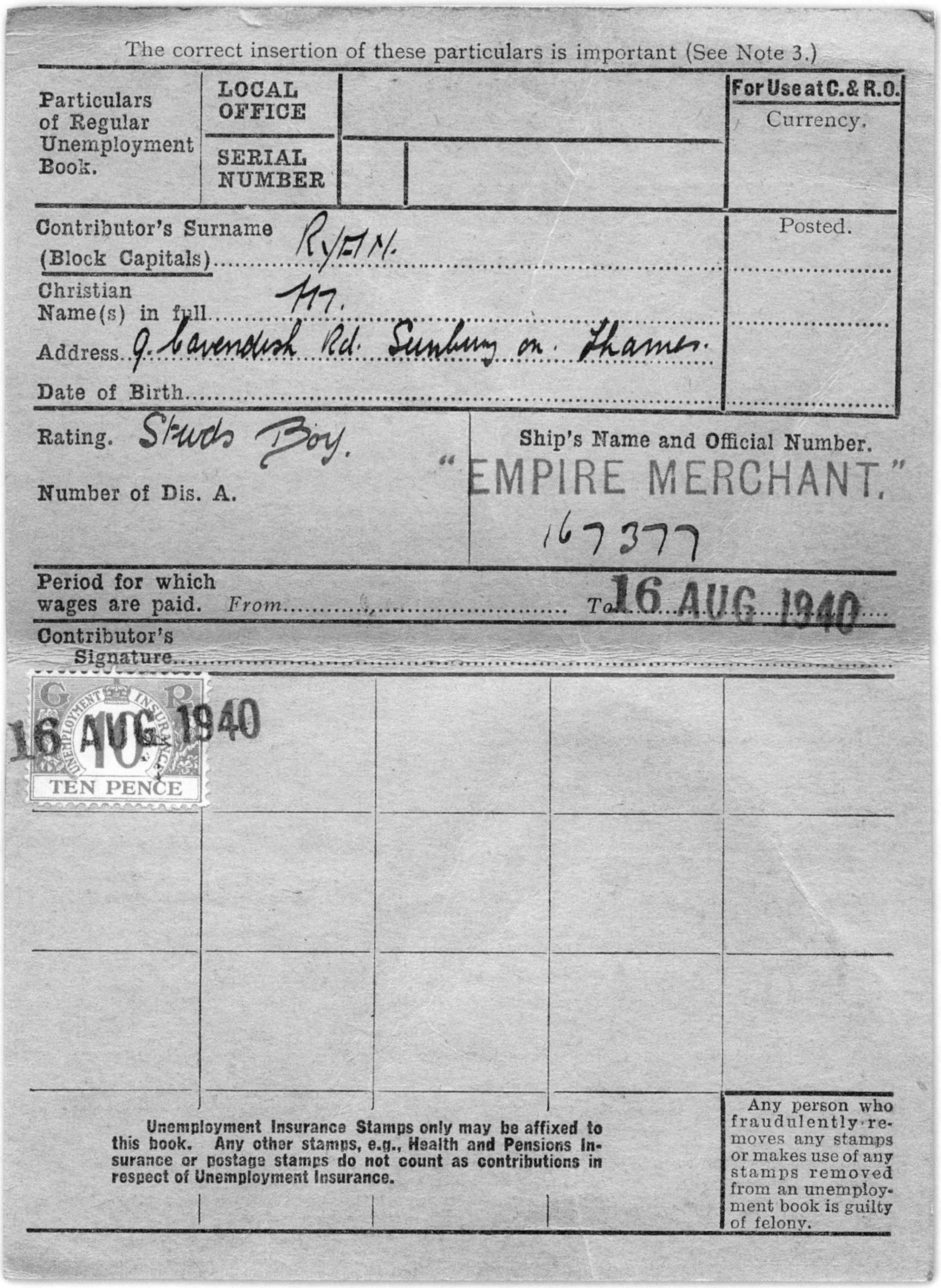

The correct insertion of these particulars is important (See Note 3.)

Particulars of Regular Unemployment Book.	LOCAL OFFICE			For Use at C. & R.O. Currency.
	SERIAL NUMBER			

Contributor's Surname (Block Capitals)	*RYAN.*		Posted.
Christian Name(s) in full	*M.*		
Address	*9. Cavendish Rd. Sunbury on Thames.*		
Date of Birth			

Rating. *Studs Boy.*

Number of Dis. A.

Ship's Name and Official Number.

" EMPIRE MERCHANT."

167377

Period for which wages are paid. *From* .... *To* **16 AUG 1940**

Contributor's Signature

16 AUG 1940
10 TEN PENCE

Unemployment Insurance Stamps only may be affixed to this book. Any other stamps, e.g., Health and Pensions Insurance or postage stamps do not count as contributions in respect of Unemployment Insurance.

Any person who fraudulently removes any stamps or makes use of any stamps removed from an unemployment book is guilty of felony.

Maurice Ryan's temporary unemployment book, showing the date his ship was sunk and the fact that his wages stopped on 16 August 1940. He was paid nothing for enduring six days in the lifeboat.

Despite his lucky escape, Maurice was determined to get back to sea.

The ships I was on were bringing grain back from Canada and also tanks and parts of planes from America. We really felt we were playing a good part and we used to get so much respect when we came back to England for doing this. Sometimes we were in a big convoy, and people don't realise this, but some of these convoys, forty, forty-two ships, stretched out for miles. They put balloons up different heights to stop dive-bombers. It makes you feel safe because most of the convoy got through. It was a spectacle. I reckon that's a majestic sight. Sometimes when you were out in the deep sea you'd get a

In convoys the slow, coal-burning ships were often the most vulnerable because they struggled to keep up with the rest. *(IWM HU3349)*

straggler, coal-burning boats mostly in them days, and they couldn't keep up but the escort can't leave the convoy. Then a couple of hours later you'd see a column of smoke go up and that would be the straggler, torpedoed. That was terrible. You'd lost one of the family. Even though she was at the arse end of the convoy, it's a loss. It took some getting over really, and you'd say, 'That's one gone already.' You don't like to lose any one of the convoy because it was so important to bring food and grain back, and so we used to feel it. But we did feel proud to be part of the Merchant Navy.

John Salinas and his wife Dorothy.

JOHN SALINAS

I was a merchant seaman on a ship in Singapore when war broke out. Very few people had a radio and there was only one on board the ship that I was on, so we were gathered round, listening to the news. There was a sense of gloom aboard the ship. I was in charge of the ship's hospital at the time and I had access to the dispensary, so we made a drink out of the alcohol which cheered us up a bit. We were all very aware of the efficiency of the Germans and they had a good historical name as a fighting race. We knew all about submarines and torpedoes from the First World War, so we knew that we were going to be very much involved in it.

The merchant ships used to sail in convoy and there were meetings when all the ships' captains went to the Admiralty and got all their instructions. One ship carried the commodore who was in charge of the convoy and it was he who transmitted all the signals from his ship. Any messages that came were sent by flag and they would hoist a string of flags up. Then the next ship would hoist the same signal so the message was passed on to the other ships. All this was very interesting for us because normally you don't have anything interesting to look at when you're at sea. The other thing you used to signal was the Aldis lamp, which went 'click, click, click'. So you began to learn the Morse code which was good fun.

In 1942 I was on a boat called the *Ville de Rouen*, a French boat. I was in catering and was Second Steward at the time. I looked after the stores. We were only about five days at sea and I was in my room when the alarm went, so I bolted up to my station which was on the poop. We had a 4.7-inch gun up there, just a defensive weapon. The night was calm, we seemed to be almost still and there were star shells in the sky. The corvettes and destroyers used to fire star shells to try and stop submarines from surfacing. The convoy I was in was a 7-knot convoy, that's the fastest speed of the slowest ship, and we hardly seemed to be moving. I was looking over the taft rail, that's the rail that goes right round the stern, and I saw two torpedoes flash by, the wake of them, just like whipping a rope up out of the water. I turned round and got on the phone to the bridge, and I hardly had time to get the words out when a third one hit us. That's quite frightening because you don't know at that time what's going to happen. Sometimes a ship will go down very quickly. Other times, because of the strength of the bulkheads, she'll stay afloat for quite a time. So once the ship was hit, it was general then to abandon ship. That's what happened in this case.

An aerial view of an Atlantic convoy showing the sheer scale of the fleet. *(IWM C2647)*

The ship seemed to steady all right. It's dark and we start lowering the lifeboats. As each boat was lowered, they rowed away from the ship and waited for the others to be lowered down. In the boat I was in there was an old bosun and myself, and a Chinaman. We were the last on the ship. We lowered our boat into the water and we got in. It was filling water and this was a bit frightening. We were baling out, baling out, but the water wasn't going down. Then the old bosun says, 'See if the plug's shipped.' All lifeboats have a plug in them and it's always left out in order to let rain water out. So we put the plug in and baled out some more and then made our way over to where the other boats were gathered. Meanwhile the ship was going down slowly in the dark and the captain had taken his uniform jacket off and was wearing a sweater, because submarines had a habit of taking senior officers off the boats and taking them as prisoners to Germany.

In the distance we could still see the convoy under attack, going away from us. There were forty-six ships and we were the sixteenth to be sunk. There were eventually twenty-three sunk altogether. Anyway, it was quiet and all of a sudden we heard the noise of the engines of a submarine. It seemed to fill the air and it

John Salinas's discharge book. The fifth entry shows when the *Ville de Rouen* was sunk – Engagement, Glasgow 7/12/42. Discharge, At Sea 28/12/42.

was coming towards us. Then it stopped and then it started again, but it started to recede. We were very pleased that it was going away because they didn't have a good record, the Germans, with mariners in boats. Then we realised why it had left because a corvette named the *Shediac* arrived on the scene and obviously the submarine had gone away to avoid that. The *Shediac* picked us up. They threw rope netting over the side and we scrambled aboard. Being in a convoy saved our lives because if we hadn't been in a convoy, there wouldn't have been a corvette to pick us up. We would have had to sail to Ireland and that's no joke at any time. Also, the submarine could have had their way with us and I don't know what they would have done because they were quite capable of running a lifeboat down or shooting the survivors. They had quite a reputation for it.

We were taken to the Azores and eventually a passenger ship came and picked us up and delivered us to Liverpool. I had a pair of sea boots on and a patrol coat and I got a taxi home. I rang the bell and my mother came to the door. She was a funny woman, my mother. She opened the door and said, 'Are you home again then?' Then turned around and walked inside. She probably thought, 'How long is he home for now? I've got to keep him fed!' If your ship was torpedoed that was the end of that and your pay was stopped. In your discharge book it shows where you were engaged, where you were discharged and what kind of a person you were. If you were sunk at sea, it was written in your discharge book. That's what it says in mine – Engaged, Liverpool. Discharged, At sea.

In 1942 I was on the *Troilus* and we went to Malta in a convoy called Harpoon. The night before we left we had a party at my house and in the morning we left for Malta. It was very exciting, all the colour of it. They picked six fast merchant ships, and here we were steaming through the Mediterranean, six fast ships. We were Commodore ship and we've got our escorts around us. What more exciting sight could you see than that? We knew that we when we got to Malta we had to go through narrows and there was no escape then because you come within aircraft range. I was on a gun then and if you've got a weapon it takes away all your fear because you've got something to hit back with. As weapons go it wasn't something magnificent. It was a Hotchkiss machine gun that I had. But the point was that I was up on deck and I had a

John Salinas sailed to Malta on the SS *Troilus*. He had great success manning one of the ship's guns.

weapon. Planes had to come in low to drop their torpedoes and when they were coming in you could really get at them. We used to fire what they called TITA. The bullets were laid out on strips and TITA stood for tracer, incendiary, tracer, armour-piercing. Because of the tracers, you did what they called hosepipe firing. You didn't need to look through the sights on the gun because you could see your stuff going through the air right to where it was going. So you could really get a good aim and accurate firing.

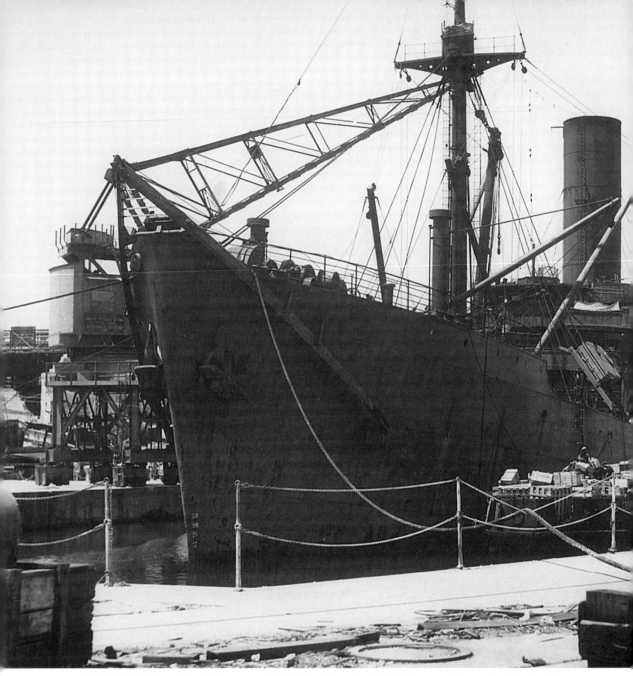

The SS *Troilus* unloads her cargo in Malta, August 1943. She was the only ship in the convoy to escape damage. *(IWM A10410)*

When the attack was on, it was really exciting. First of all you have a screen of destroyers and their job is to keep the planes away from you. They're guarding you and my goodness they've got some weapons. They had what they call multiple pom-poms and they could put some stuff into the sky. But every so often a plane would get through and there was nothing then between that plane

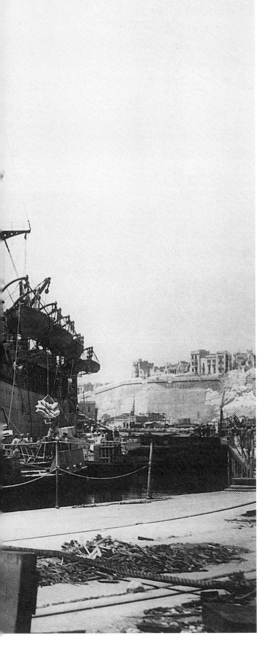

and you. Then the Bofors guns would go. They were the biggest anti-aircraft guns we had – they would fire 14mm shells. They could pump out shells at 120 a minute and they would start up, 'boom, boom, boom, boom'. Then as it got closer the Oerlikons would start and they chattered. They were about 600 rounds a minute, 'rararararara'. And the sound is building up and the fella on the stern would let go one of his with an enormous bang. Then it came within your range. There was a tremendous cacophony of sound, it was terribly exciting and all of a sudden you would see the plane engine start to roast, start to get hot, hot, glow, glow, and then she'd tip over and the wing would hit the water and she'd go helter-skelter. I mean, when can you match that for excitement.

We were credited with shooting down four planes on that convoy. When we got home each gunner got twenty-three quid because you got prize money. Very nice thank you. But on that convoy most of the ships were sunk. Eleven left Alexandria at the far end and six came though Gibraltar, and out of those seventeen ships, the only ship that got in untouched was the one I was on. But going into Malta was very, very thrilling, because all the population were on the sea wall at Valetta cheering. We were glad we were in because we were out of the battle and as soon as we arrived they lit smoke bombs to hide us from the planes. We went into Malta at the beginning of June and we didn't get out until August because it was just as hard to get out as it was to get in. But we were aware of how important it was to get through because all this activity was all tied up with El Alamein. Montgomery was at one side, building up for El Alamein, and Rommel was at the other, and Rommel's supplies were constantly being attacked from Malta. Malta was like a big aircraft carrier and we were attacking supplies going across from Italy and Sicily to North Africa, so it had a big bearing on the war.

Crewmen stand on the hull of HMS *Barham* as she capsizes after being struck by three torpedoes from German submarine U-331. Seconds later she exploded, with the loss of over 860 men. *(IWM MOI FLM 1985)*

In 1944 I was in the English Channel, coming back from France. The sea was calm and I was kneeling on my bunk watching doodlebugs coming over when the ship was hit. I'd like to know how it happened because there must have been very few ships sunk after D-Day in the Channel, very few indeed because we had total control, except for this little torpedo boat that got us! We were hit forward of the bridge, the best place you could be hit. Of course she shudders, stops and then starts to tilt. Well, I jumped off the bunk and I couldn't find the bloody door. I knew where the door was, but I couldn't find it, and when I did find the handle, I can't tell you what a relief it was. I went up on deck and everybody's gathering, beginning to get the boats out. Then I realised I'd left a photograph of Dorothy, my wife, in my cabin. I'd had it with me through the war, on every ship, and I just felt that I wasn't going to lose it, I just wanted the picture.

So against all common sense I went back down again for it. On the way down I was thinking, 'You're a bloody fool', because like I said, you don't know how a ship is going to behave when she's hit. I got the photograph; it was laying on its face on the desk in my cabin. I climbed back up because the ship was now tilted and it's surprisingly harder to go up a companion way when it's tilted like that than when it's level. I got on deck and I reprimanded myself for being such a fool because I could have lost my life. Then I got into the lifeboat and we launched, got away and watched the ship go down. Then we were picked up by a fishing boat and delivered to port. But I got the picture and I've still got it today.

The precious photo of Dorothy which John Salinas risked his life to save.

CYRIL STEPHENS

When I was a boy I worked as a gardener. Then I trained as a painter and decorator, and it was during that time that the war started and I was conscripted. I'd lost two uncles who were in the Army in the First World War and I thought I didn't want to go the same way as them. I also thought there would be a lot of kit to carry in the Army, so I thought if I joined the Navy, once I get on board the ship there wouldn't be much kit to carry around. So I joined the Navy. My family worked on the farm, so I had no connection whatsoever with the Navy. The first time I ever saw the sea was the Bristol Channel at Weston-Super-Mare! Anyway we did about ten weeks training, all this square bashing which I could never understand, and we did seamanship, knots and splices, flags and cordage, just a brief knowledge. But we were all bookies' runners, chippies, bricklayers, carpenters, painters. We were supposed to be seamen but we never had a clue what it was all about! Then we got a draft to pick up a corvette in Belfast, called HMS *Orchis*. A pretty little thing she was, a pale grey and blue. Of course, not having been in the Navy long, I hadn't really seen any big ships, but the old hands who had been on bigger ships were more or less disgusted to think that they came down from a big ship to this little thing because she was only 950 tons. We put to sea after about a fortnight and well, I thought I was going to die to tell you the honest truth. I thought, my God, what have I joined?

I was always seasick for the first three days at sea and it's one of the most unpleasant things there is in life, I should imagine, to be seasick. These little corvettes, they'd bounce like a cork on water. I think the best way to describe a corvette is like a terrier with a rat. It seemed as though the sea would catch hold of them and shake them. You used to start bouncing and then you'd get this awful feeling. Your stomach doesn't seem to belong to your body somehow and all of a sudden you're sick, up it comes. You think, 'My God, I wish I was dead.'

'Like a terrier with a rat': Cyril Stephens' memory of the conditions on board the tiny corvettes is graphically captured in this photograph. *(IWM PL2145A)*

But after about three days, you got over it. The thing could stand on its head and you wouldn't take any notice.

But although you were seasick, you still had your duties to perform. One of the jobs that was bad was when you went on to the wheel. You had a little tiny magnetic compass and there was a line that represented the ship's head. Provided you swung the same degrees either side of the ship's head, you were on course. And I can always remember there was a stanchion next to you with a bucket tied to it where you were sick in. When I think now that the only thing I was capable of steering was a bicycle and there you was out in the middle of the Atlantic, in the middle of a bally convoy, trying to steer a corvette! It's ridiculous really. But in the end you got confident and you could do the job.

If you were on watch and you were detailed masthead look out, you started in the whale deck to climb up to this mast. Just imagine, you had a pair of sea boots on, some heavy thick socks, a dufflecoat, and if it happened to be a bit rainy you'd have an oil skin on, plus a balaclava helmet and a pair of binoculars, and you had to climb up this mast, which is absolutely vertical. It was your job then to try and spot the U-boats. But the wind used to almost cut your eyes out and one of the awful things was the fumes from the funnel. If we had a following steam, you'd get these fumes coming over which made you as sick as a dog. But it was your job to scour the horizon to see if you could see anything. I can always remember we had a lovely New Zealand officer on board and he used to say to us when we went on watch, 'If you can spot a U-boat, and we can sink it, I'll see if I can get you the VC.' We never got as lucky as that. I doubt whether you'd spot a U-boat unless it surfaced and you'd be extremely lucky to see a periscope because we were never still.

You were informed where there were packs of U-boats about. They used to shadow the convoy during the day and then creep up at night. Then all of a sudden you'd hear a terrible explosion. You'd see a tanker go up and all hell would be let loose then. I've got such admiration for the merchant fleet because if you see a torpedo hit a tanker, it's one sheet of flame and no more and you think, 'Look at the lives onboard there that's gone.' Not a snowball's chance in hell of ever getting rescued half of those people. There's an awful feeling: God, all those lives lost. It really did upset me because I thought, 'There's someone could be the son or the husband with young children at home, with no known grave, only the sea.' I thought, 'God that could have been us.' I don't think this country really honoured its debt to these merchant ships.

When we used to go into attack it might last three or four hours. Although we might not be involved ourselves, it might be right over the other side of the

convoy, but you were always there. You had to be where the senior escort told you to be. You couldn't go chasing about the bally ocean like a pack of hounds, otherwise you'd be useless. There was all this long waiting, knowing that underneath the waves somewhere was one, perhaps two U-boats, waiting. Then suddenly you got these ASDIC ratings, what we called a ping. It used to be a hit-and-miss sort of a job until you picked up this ping. This electrical impulse goes out, 'ping'. And if it hits something, it comes back, 'pong'. And the further away it is, it's 'ping . . . pong'. But as soon as it gets near it's 'ping pong, ping pong'. Soon you're almost on top of them and they say, 'Fire!' and away goes the old depth charge. When they went off it was almost as though you'd lifted the ship out of the water and dropped her. It was terrific and a great plume of water would come up. Then you search around for the U-boat, hoping to God you've got it.

Throughout the war there was a real love for the ship I was on. You'd see this little tiny corvette bouncing up and down on the waves and you'd think, 'Crikey, if she can do it, we're not gonna let her down.' And I can tell you this, when those men left those corvettes after the war they were in tears because it was their home. Suddenly to see these lovely little ships run up on the mudflats, they were in tears. I was on board for three and a half years, it was beautiful. And when you got over seasickness, the rougher the weather, the better you liked it. It was exhilarating. 'Crikey, let's get out there.' The time of my life that was. I'd never been at sea before and by God I was seasick and bad, and by God I was ill, but I wouldn't have changed it. I loved it.

Opposite: The corvettes were particularly successful in the battle against the U-boats. *(Courtesy of R. Conyers Nesbit)*

FIVE

D-DAY TO VICTORY

From France to Germany with the West Country's Finest

At 10.56pm on 5 June 1944 six Halifax bombers took off from an airfield in Dorset on a secret mission. Each towed a Horsa glider carrying a handful of highly trained troops from the British 6th Airborne Division upon whose shoulders the success of the D-Day invasion rested. Below them as they crossed the English Channel some 150,000 Allied troops prepared for the beach assault that was to follow, unaware that their chances of survival lay, to some extent, in the hands of the men who flew overhead. For if the invasion were to be successful, these airborne forces would have to capture intact the two vitally important bridges which crossed the Caen Canal and River Orne in a swift and silent *coup de main*. With these bridges safely in British hands, the Germans could be prevented from launching the 21st Panzer Division in a major counter-assault, which if mobilised quickly, had the potential to trap Allied forces on the beaches with devastating consequences. It was essential that the bridges, once captured, were held at all costs, despite the fact that German retaliation was expected before reinforcements from the Parachute Regiment could arrive. But providing all went according to plan, the Paras would be able to link up with the Commandos of Lord Lovat's 1st Special Service Brigade, who were preparing to land at Sword Beach, and with this bridgehead intact, the breakout from the beaches could begin. It was a huge task, and as the gliders approached their target, young officer David Wood sat gripping the arm of the man next to him, waiting for the impact of landing. Within minutes, he would be leading his platoon into what would become one of the most celebrated acts of the war: the capture of Pegasus Bridge.

As dawn broke on 6 June, battleships in the Channel began to pound the Normandy coastline with shells from their heavy guns and at 0725 hours, 30,000 troops of the British 3rd Infantry Division began their

Airborne troops inside a Horsa glider like the one David Wood flew in en route to Pegasus Bridge. *(IWM CH10208)*

assault upon Sword Beach. Waiting just offshore was junior officer Ken Davenport with the 5th Battalion, The King's Regiment. His men were designated as Beach Group and were given the unenviable task of clearing the beaches of obstacles, vehicles and, of course, bodies to allow those following in subsequent waves to have a swift and safe exit from the shore. It was to be a difficult and dangerous role: they were landing just an hour behind the first wave of assault troops and fighting was still likely to be fierce. But as he stood in his Landing Craft Assault, ploughing towards the coast, Ken tried to hold back the fear and focus on the job in hand. At 08.15 hours the landing ramp on Ken's boat crashed into the water: his D-Day had begun. Twenty-five minutes later, Lord Lovat arrived on the beach and his Commandos made their way ashore to

Following spread: Troops land on Sword Beach on the morning of 6 June 1944. *(IWM B5114)*

the sound of bagpipes, played by Bill Millin. Several hours later, it was the welcome sound of the pipes that announced Lovat's arrival to David Wood and the men on Pegasus Bridge and by 1300 hours the planned link-up between the 6th Airborne and the 3rd Infantry Division was achieved. For David it was a moment tinged with sadness, for in the action to capture the bridge his good friend Den Brotheridge had become the first Allied soldier to be killed by enemy action that day.

With D-Day an overwhelming success, Allied forces could now begin the breakout through Normandy. On D-Day plus 17, Geoff Young landed on Gold Beach with the 4th Battalion, The Wiltshire Regiment, part of the 43rd Wessex Division, which was to help with the push through France. Formed as a West Country Territorial Army Division before the First World War, the Fighting Wyverns, as they were known were made up of part-time soldiers from the ancient Kingdom of Wessex, including men from Somerset, Wiltshire and Gloucestershire. When they sailed for France in June 1944, they were generally believed to be the most highly trained infantry division ever to leave British shores. They had to be. In the ten months that followed, the Wessex Division was involved in every major operation undertaken by the British 2nd Army. Within weeks of arriving in Normandy, the division was involved in one of the bloodiest battles of the campaign, the fight for Hill 112, during which they lost more than 2,000 men in just 36 hours. But they fought on and after succeeding in the breakout from Normandy, the 43rd Wessex saw action in the crossing of the River Seine, in Holland during the famous battles at Arnhem and Nijmegen and in the advance through Germany. When ceasefire was declared on 4 May 1945, soldiers of the division were the furthest forward of any in the British 2nd Army, but the cost of their victory was unprecedented. During their time in action they had suffered over 12,000 casualties, the highest casualty rate of any division in the 2nd Army. But for Geoff Young, there was to be a happy conclusion to the war, and one which in many ways signified that old differences could now perhaps be forgotten, and peace be brought to Europe.

DAVID WOOD

I was born in 1923 in Corsham in Wiltshire, but we moved to Bath, where I went to Monkton Combe school. I was in the Army class, which trained us to enter the Royal Military Academy at Sandhurst, but the war came along and Sandhurst packed up. So when I was 18½ I joined the Army and went to an officer cadet training unit at Dunbar in Scotland. Halfway through the course

David Wood.

we were asked which regiments we'd like to be commissioned into, so I chose, in order, Wiltshire, Somerset and Gloucestershire, only to be told on the day that we were given our posting orders that I was going to the Oxfordshire and Buckinghamshire Light Infantry Regiment, of which I'd never heard. But they were building up what they called the Air Landing Battalions and I was posted to what we called the 52nd at Basingstoke, where I joined Major John Howard's Company as Platoon Commander of No.24 Platoon. John Howard was a perfectionist. He was a very good trainer. He was very hard and I think that I could say he was fair. He never asked us to do anything he couldn't do himself, and probably do better. But there wasn't any room for sloppiness or anything of that sort. His standards were of the highest and he was determined that his company was going to be the best in the battalion, which I like to think it was because we were the ones selected to go on the *coup de main* operation subsequently.

Having rehearsed on the playing fields behind Bulford Camp, we moved down to Exeter with our Royal Engineers as a *coup de main* party of six platoons. Someone had discovered that there were two bridges very similar to the ones we were going to attack, one over the Exeter Canal and one over the River Exe. We spent three days and three nights attacking those bridges in every possible and impossible combination. At the end of our stay there was a hiccup because the company second-in-command, Captain Priday, paid the men out a day earlier

Major John Howard earned great respect from his men.

than usual and they went into Exeter where they drank rather too much and there was some damage done. But this was all smoothed over by John Howard, who was an ex-policeman, and the police officer in charge of Exeter City, who was himself a First World War soldier, so they got out of that.

After rehearsals down in Exeter, we moved into what we called a transit camp near a small airfield at Tarrant Rushton in Dorset. There we were secured in and nobody was allowed in or out because it was then and only then that we were told where we were going and exactly what we were going to do. John Howard gave out his orders, which he had received from the brigadier of the Parachute Regiment, under whose command we went into action. Then we as platoon commanders went into a briefing tent, which was guarded by Military Police, in which there was the most detailed model you could imagine of our objectives, with every slit trench, every building all faithfully represented. Each platoon had its specific task and mine, as the second glider to land at what is now called Pegasus Bridge, was to clear the inner defences: to go across the road and put out of action the Germans who were in dugouts or slit trenches and make our way up to the canal bank. I knew exactly what I had to do and that's what I briefed my platoon that they had to do.

An aerial photograph showing the bridges over the Caen Canal (bottom) and the River Orne (middle). The gliders that carried David Wood and his colleagues can be clearly seen. At the top of the picture are gliders that landed later at the drop zone near the village of Ranville. *(IWM MH24891)*

A platoon was made up of a scout section and two rifle sections, so each was given its task and knew exactly what was expected of it. In the meantime, it was made absolutely clear that we might not land where we expected to, or in the order that we planned, so we might have to do somebody else's task. Of course the soldiers were encouraged to ask questions and at one stage one of the soldiers said, 'Can we have a doctor?' He had realised that we were going into action unsupported, at least for the time being, and we could get wounded and there wouldn't be anybody to look after us. John Howard took the point and within 24 hours we had a doctor who'd never been in a glider in his life!

Having been given our orders, we were visited by at least two brigadiers who made it absolutely clear to us that what we were doing was vital. The two

The bridge over the Caen Canal, later renamed Pegasus Bridge after the winged horse which is the emblem of the 6th Airborne Division. The first building on the left-hand side of the bridge is the Café Gondrée.

bridges were on the eastern flank of the whole Operation Overlord, and if those bridges had been lost, or not captured intact, it would have enabled the enemy to counter-attack in a far more dangerous way than he was able to do. There was never any doubt, no room at all for the idea that we shouldn't succeed. I suppose in our own minds we must have had some question marks because we were going in at night, into enemy territory, we were going in a glider which once it had been cast off had no option but to come down and land. So there might have been some doubts but we certainly didn't talk about them. I've heard since that somebody said we all knew we were going on a suicide mission, but, forgive me, that's utter rubbish. We never thought that at all. We thought we were going on a vitally important mission and that we were going to make a success of it.

Horsa Bridge, which spans the River Orne. *(IWM B5230)*

David Wood felt he couldn't go into battle without his tie.

On 4 June there was a false alarm and the whole thing was delayed by 24 hours. This was a great disappointment because we'd been keyed up for what we were going to do. We'd had our final briefing and we'd tested our weapons and blacked our faces and loaded our magazines, and we went through all that and then it was postponed. The next day the operation was back on and I was unable to find my tie. Now, you may feel that a tie is of no real importance, but I didn't feel that I could go into action without one. We had a couple of Canadian officers with us who were there specifically in case one of us fell out, to take our places and this Canadian officer said, 'You can have my tie, Dave.' To my astonishment he unhooked his made-up khaki tie, with elastic, and gave it to me to wear. So I felt properly dressed for going into action! Having tested our weapons and loaded up and so on, we moved in individual trucks to the six gliders. When we got there, we emplaned through the two doors which the glider has and sat down either side, rather like in an old-fashioned tram, with a belt securing us into our seats and, of course, the two pilots up in front, who were going to get us where we needed to go. John Howard came round and said goodbye and wished us the best of luck. The up-and-over doors were then shut. There was a Halifax bomber on the runway with its engines revving and the tow-rope between us; it tightened and we were airborne. I think the glider gets airborne slightly before the bomber does as a matter of fact. We took off at 1056 and flew for about an hour and 20 minutes. It was normal that we sang and so we started singing in the glider, but then for some reason we went quiet. It's been suggested that it was because we thought the enemy might hear us singing and there would be problems, but anyway, it wasn't a noisy flight from our point of view at all. The Halifax pilots had found a way through the flak, so we were not under fire at all during that particular flight.

We were cast off between 4,000 and 6,000 feet and glid, if that's the word, for about 7 minutes. You don't really hear anything until the doors are opened. Then the doors were opened, one at the front and one at the back, for us to make a quick exit because that's what we were really frightened about – that once we landed, if the enemy were alert we'd have been under fire and there's nothing worse than being in a glider, sitting on the ground under automatic fire. There was an eerie feeling once the doors were opened because, of course, it was completely silent and the air was swishing past the side of the glider. I didn't stand up and look where we were going. I was sitting there, holding on to the chap next to me as firmly as I could when quite suddenly, one of the pilots said, 'Christ, there's the bridge.' Then he put the nose of the glider down very steeply and we came in at about 90mph.

We lost our wheels on the first bump and so the glider skidded along on its bottom and that caused sparks to come up from the ground. There were flints

The first three gliders landed accurately on the banks of the Caen Canal. Pegasus Bridge is just behind the trees – landing the gliders this close in the darkness took incredible skill. Air Chief Marshal Leigh-Mallory described it as the greatest feat of flying of the Second World War. *(IWM B5233)*

on the ground and we thought that we were under fire. We made a very hard landing and I was thrown out through the side of the glider, complete with my Sten gun and a canvas bucket of grenades that I'd taken in order to have enough ammunition. Not a very sensible thing to do. Both I and the grenades survived but I was a bit dazed. We knew exactly what we had to do. We had rehearsed it *ad nauseam* and so we just got on with it. We assembled as we'd practised doing before – under the wings of the glider – and when it was reported to me that everybody was present, we doubled forward to report to Major Howard who had landed No.1 and who was crouched by the barbed wire just near the bridge. He whispered to me, 'Number two, David,' and I knew what number two was: that was to go and clear the inner defences.

I led my platoon across the road and we were probably doing rather too much firing because it was our first time in action. We were also shouting, which was part of the drill to identify one platoon from another. So my platoon went across the road shouting 'Charlie, Charlie, Charlie' as loudly as they could to identify us. We cleared out the dugouts and trenches as far as we could see in the dark. I came across a German machine gun with a full belt of ammunition on it. I didn't see the man who might have been firing it. We recovered some boxes of ammunition and that sort of thing. We threw grenades into the slit trenches and dugouts in case they were there – the garrison was some fifty strong and obviously there were men asleep and off duty because there were only sentries on the two bridges.

I had succeeded, or so I thought, in clearing the inner defences when over the small radio which every platoon carried came the two magic words 'Ham' and 'Jam', which were the two success signals for the two bridges. So I knew that by then we had captured both bridges intact and that took place within 10 minutes of landing with very small casualties. We were excited at that news and chuffed, to use an old Army word: morale couldn't have been higher.

It was a remarkably successful operation, largely I think because we achieved complete surprise. I must put in a word for the Royal Engineers because they went in with us and I've always said they had the most unenviable task of anybody: they had to crawl under the two bridges, knowing that they were mined and not knowing whether somebody in the pillbox could press a button and blow them absolutely sky high.

John Howard ordered me to report to him for fresh orders, so I moved back towards the road with my platoon sergeant and my orderly. Then I was hit in the left leg by a burst of Schmeisser machine pistol. I never saw the chap who did it, but he must have been remarkably close because three bullets went into my left leg. You feel nothing, actually, you just go down. I'd heard all sorts of marvellous stories about John Wayne cracking about with one leg as if nothing had happened. It's not like that at all. You're totally useless. Actually, I was frightened. I wasn't frightened in the glider and I wasn't frightened when I was carrying out the actual attack, but when I was lying on the ground, and the grass was quite long there and it was dark, I thought any minute this chap would come and finish me off. So I shouted and very quickly two of the platoon medical orderlies, who I'm glad to say I'd trained to do their job properly, came along and put a rifle splint on my left leg and jabbed some morphine into me. I lay on a stretcher which somebody found and the doctor came and looked at me, but there was so much going on they hadn't got time to do more than that. Between the two bridges it had been decided there should be a casualty clearing post, so eventually, somewhere nearer daylight, I was carried there.

The word went round very quickly that Den Brotheridge had been hit and then he and I were in the casualty clearing post at the same time. He died there. I never spoke to him. In fact, I don't think that anybody, apart from the chaps who were immediately round him when he was shot, were able to speak to him. They obviously went to his assistance straight away and asked him all the sort of questions you normally ask, but I doubt if he could answer because he was shot in the neck and it was a mortal wound. It was one of saddest moments, of course. He was a great friend of mine; we lived in the same billet and everything. We obviously knew there were going to be

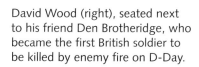

David Wood (right), seated next to his friend Den Brotheridge, who became the first British soldier to be killed by enemy fire on D-Day.

Snipers in the church tower in the nearby village of Le Port were dealt with by a shot from an anti-tank rifle. *(IWM B5429)*

casualties, but he was really the first one, apart from the lance corporal who was thrown out of the glider. It was a major blow that we'd lost him so early.

When daylight came there were problems with snipers; the Germans had snipers in the church tower at Le Port and on the roof of a maternity home on the other side of the canal. I was minding my own business and really not taking much interest in life at that moment when there was a bang and a bullet thudded into the ground by my head. I thought, 'Well, that's it, he'll never miss me a second time.' I looked up and the splendid corporal in the Royal Army Medical Corps who we took with us, and who was looking after me, had drawn his pistol to protect his patient, had accidentally discharged it and very nearly shot me. I've always felt since that it's not a good idea to arm doctors and that it would be better if they looked after their patients without weapons! Some of the other casualties ended up at the Pegasus Bridge café, the Café Gondrée, where the owner dug up ninety-seven bottles of champagne which he dished out to the wounded and the non-wounded, I think. I never got a drop of that and I always felt rather hurt about it later on.

Whilst I was lying there, before they moved me, two things happened that I remember. One was that the counter-attack had begun. We were worried about counter-attacks because it was one thing to capture the bridges, but quite another to be sure that we could hold on to them. These three armoured cars came down across Pegasus Bridge, or attempted to, from the village of Le Port. Sergeant 'Wagger' Thornton of one of the platoons had a PIAT, a projector infantry anti-tank weapon, and he waited and waited and finally fired one shot. He hit the first armoured car spot on. It was like a firework display and I could see that lying on my stretcher. The other thing that happened was this tale about the commandos coming up the canal after Lord Lovat with their piper, Bill Millin, who it is quite true to say played the pipes both on the beaches earlier and as he came up the path with the commandos to relieve us. I heard the pipes, although I didn't really believe that it could be pipes.

It was the task of the 7th Battalion of the Parachute Regiment to relieve us on the bridges, but their problem was that they were blown all over the place. They

Lord Lovat's commandos land at Sword Beach, with piper Bill Millin in the foreground. The pipes were a welcome sound for David Wood. *(IWM B5103)*

British troops cross Pegasus Bridge, in the days following D-Day. The gliders are visible behind the trees. *(IWM B5287)*

assembled eventually and came to relieve us. Very welcome they were too. It was a good sight to see them coming down because initially, not for very long, but initially we were simply on our tod and had to get on with it. Our chaps had a few cracks about, 'Where had they been?' and 'Had they enjoyed their 48 hours leave?' and that sort of thing. But of course we were delighted to see them and they were very quickly involved in action up in the villages of Bénouville and Le Port.

We didn't see anything of the actual seaborne assault, it was too far away. The only indication I had that anything was happening was from the gunfire from the heavy ships. There was a ship out there called *Warspite* that fired 16-inch shells and they were terrifying. They went over our heads, I'm glad to say, and I'm sure they were hitting the targets they were aimed at, but I've never been under the track of a heavy shell before. That was rewarding, one felt, 'Good-o, they're there, they're coming.'

I was very proud, and still am, of having taken part in what was such a vital operation. I learnt to sort of grow out of it a bit because I spent thirty-six years in the

Army. But it was a very successful operation and I think that was really because firstly, we had a very simple plan. Secondly, we achieved complete surprise. And not least because we carried it out with such spirit and élan. We were going to capture those two bridges and indeed we did. But being wounded and unable to take any further part, there was an acute feeling of disappointment. I'd had my platoon for two years and only three men in it had changed in that time. The one thing I wanted to do was to lead my platoon in action and to prove myself as a platoon commander. I suppose to a certain extent I did that in the initial assault, but I would have given anything to go on commanding them over the period that was to follow, when, of course, I couldn't. I suppose if you are a realist, I was lucky in a way because after 25 minutes I was out of action. Next day, and in the next few days, the company had a very busy time up in the villages of Escoville and Hérouvillette where they lost over sixty out of action. I might easily been one of those.

David Wood (right) and John Howard share a drink with Monsieur Gondrée at the Café Gondrée in 1946. David Wood's injury on D-Day meant he missed out on the champagne!

Ken Davenport was a young officer with the 5th Battalion, The King's Regiment, who were responsible for clearing Sword Beach on D-Day.

KEN DAVENPORT

I was commissioned as a very raw 2nd lieutenant (with 5th Battalion, The King's Regiment) in 1943. I was posted up to Ayr for pre-invasion training where we did landings from the sea on to the coast under live fire from our own chaps. One of our fellows was killed during one of those landings. We were there for about six months, I suppose, and after that I was posted to Inverness. Then we went down to the holding camp, just at the back of Portsmouth. When we knew we were going down to the holding camp ready for embarkation somewhere, nobody knew where of course, there was excitement, no fear or anything like that, but excitement at what it would be like, where it would be and when.

The officers who needed to know were shown plans, large-scale maps of the exact objectives we were making for in Normandy. Sword Beach was our landing area. I was the intelligence officer at the time and my objective was to find a certain orchard, dig in there and establish a network of communications, field telephones and that sort of thing. We were in the camp for ten or fourteen days. We were called forward on 5 June, of course, and assigned an LSI, a Landing Ship Infantry, on which our LCA, Landing Craft Assault, was berthed. We were then told there was a delay of 24 hours, so we had 24 hours to hang around.

We had our own padre and on the night before the invasion we had a large service. There were hundreds of soldiery there, most of them Christian or religious in their way, or they became religious on the way over to France. You did see the odd prayer being said by the odd soldier in the corner of the craft as we were ploughing toward the coast and I said the odd inward prayer. We took off from Havant and the ship I was on held 700 troops and about fourteen or sixteen Landing Craft Assault, one of which was assigned to my platoon. Obviously there was an awful lot of tenseness. We knew what we were in for by now. We knew what the obstacles were and we knew more or less the strength of the opposition; pillboxes, barbed-wire entanglements, mines strapped to the top of posts to blow up the assault craft as they landed and things like that. Up to that point I think it had been a bit of an adventure for most of the men, excitement certainly. We were gonna fight the baddies.

Once the LCA had been lowered on to the sea the coast was very visible and you could see our own guns firing from the battleships and cruisers, softening up the opposition before we landed. The noise was absolutely deafening. It was the most marvellous sight you'd ever seen. Then we saw planes and gliders going over and it was a heartening sight. There were flocks of them on our east. That lifted your spirits, to know that those boys up there are going to do something to help you when you get ashore. They'd be knocking out a lot of the opposition. The very fact that our own air force had supremacy of the air – if they hadn't had been there, we wouldn't have landed, we wouldn't have even touched down.

My batman, Bill Carpenter, was on the LCA with me. He was an old soldier who joined up when he was a boy and he was much above the allowable age for D-Day really, but he wanted to be with his officer, he wanted to be with me. We'd established a bit of a rapport during the ten months we'd known one another. Anyway, we'd just taken off from the ship on to the open sea and were about halfway to the shore when Bill appeared with a cake which he'd brought with him. All the men looked at him in amazement: 'What the hell's Carpenter doing with a cake?' So he cut it up and we all had a piece of cake and were munching cake about half an hour before we landed. I thought, 'Well, if my batman can feel that sang-froid, who am I, his officer, to feel dithery?' And it bucked one up a bit, a little bit, just enough to keep you going. But as we approached the land, I had a sort of numb fear that deadened any worries I might have had. The nearer you got, the more blasé you became and I certainly didn't think that I'd be killed. We'd had very long instruction on what to expect, but as we got nearer I think then the men must have felt like I did. You knew quite clearly where you were going, what you were doing. You knew there were bullets over there and a tank over there and you saw your own landing craft being hit and men being thrown into the water. But it was this last-minute feeling that you're not going to get killed.

I ordered the ramp down and down it came. We were in about 3 feet of water and every man had been told to keep his rifle above his head to keep it dry. We were about 10 feet from dry land and we waded ashore. There were lots of flashes from pillboxes and strongpoints that were located on the water's edge on the embankment, about 100 yards away. They were firing incessantly. On Sword Beach there were very heavily fortified pillboxes, about 4 or 5 feet thick concrete, containing machine guns, anti-tank guns, and that's where most of the danger came from. Occasionally you got a hell of a blast from the Moaning Minnies, as we called them, on the heights left and right, which were enfilading

The view approaching Sword Beach on D-Day as Ken Davenport would have seen it. *(IWM B5102)*

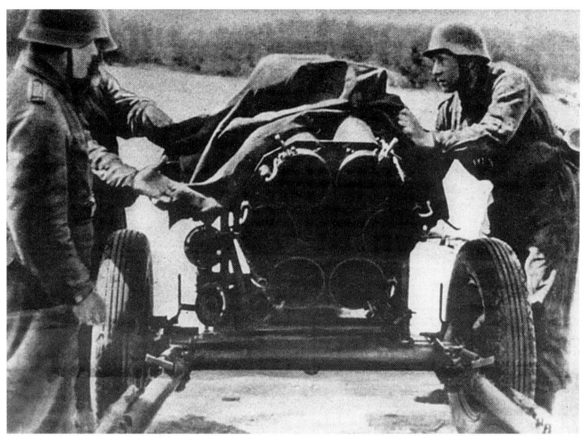

German troops prepare the dreaded *Nebelwerfer,* nicknamed 'Moaning Minnies' because of the sound they made. These caused a great deal of damage on D-Day and later for the 43rd Wessex Division at Hill 112. *(IWM STT2617)*

the beach. They were six-barrelled things, dreadful things and when they were fired they made a terrible moan. There was a kind of Bofors gun up on the left that was a damn nuisance because that was knocking our chaps out. Bodies were all over the place and tanks had gone ashore ahead of us and they were dismembered, tracks hanging off, bodies hanging out. You realised you were in the thick of it, yet the funny thing was, it was just like a film, you didn't take much notice. Your main aim was to do what you had to do. I remember there was a chap on my left – he wasn't one of mine – he was shouting, 'Help, help', but I couldn't stop. You were told not to. The medics were at the back of us anyway and they were the bravest people on that beach, I think. But you seize your objective, you don't hang about. As I said, the mind had numbed quite a bit, you felt like a robot. You'd got enough sense inside you to lead you forward

Phil Scarfe, Ken Davenport's great friend who was killed on Sword Beach as he attacked one of the German emplacements that lined the embankment.

to your objective, but you couldn't care less about what was happening either side of you. When we did a roll-call later, there were three missing. I'd lost three men out of thirty-five, which wasn't too bad.

My great friend Phil Scarfe was in command of the LCA to my left as we landed. His job was to capture two pillboxes and he'd got a platoon of thirty men to do it with. They'd got bazookas for trying to blast the stronghold. But the bow of his LCA was blown off as they landed and he lost about half of his men, I think, at that time. So what were left of his men ran up the beach. He had a revolver, which sounds a bit stupid but that's all the officers had, and he was shot about halfway up the beach. He was wounded, but he mustered his men and led the way again. Then he was then shot again and killed, but not before he'd killed one of the defenders. Within about half an hour his platoon had captured this pillbox and they massacred the buggers inside. We buried Phil above the high-water mark in a makeshift grave and very touchingly, his wife sent her wedding veil for me to put on his grave because they'd only been married about a month or two. She also asked me to be godfather to their unborn son. Phil was eventually moved into the War Graves military cemetery in Bayeux.

I was making for an exit with all my chaps and we were behind a tank. You walked in a tank track so that you weren't blown up by a mine and that was the safest place to be. The promenade was lined with very large mansions and in between there was usually an alleyway which led from the beach to the lateral road behind. We had to get through there to get to the orchard and as we went through this narrow entrance between the houses, it was too narrow for the tank and the tank gouged lines out of the walls of the houses and they're still there. We got safely across the lateral road. There was some firing, but the assault troops had rooted out all the opposition by house-to-house fighting. It was comparatively calm I suppose, so much so that there were small groups of French girls and women crouching in little alcoves with champagne, throwing flowers at us, the liberators. We didn't have time to appreciate it.

We carried on and established ourselves in this orchard which was our objective. Suddenly, a Messerschmitt came over and about 150 yards away our 3-ton ammunition truck was stationed. Three of my men were inside it, sorting out the ammunition, and it was hit and it went up like a firework display. There was not a thing we could do and the contents were exploding all over the place. There were screams and then silence. You couldn't get anywhere near this flaming inferno. One of my most harrowing experiences was later, writing to the mother of one and the wives of two, telling them what had happened. It was the officer's duty to do it for his men. In a way they were fortunate because with a lot of soldiers, you didn't know where they were killed or when.

My regiment had been chosen as what they called a beach group. We were responsible for keeping the beaches clear of everything: bodies, German and

The confusion on Sword Beach on D-Day, which Ken Davenport's battalion had to clear before the next wave of troops arrived. *(IWM B5270)*

Ken Davenport eventually helped secure the bridgehead at Sword Beach.

British, barbed-wire entanglements, dragging away the disabled tanks, lorries, the lot, clearing the beaches because the oncoming thousands of troops would have to have that space to land on. It was essential that it was cleared and that's what we were there for. That was why I was responsible for keeping in touch with our forward companies, to see what had to be done. Infantry and stores and ammunition were starting to pour in and it was a shambles. We hadn't cleared it by half when the next wave arrived because we were still being fired on of course. But eventually it cleared itself and we established a beach-head.

We were there for two or three weeks clearing up. After we'd cleared the beaches, we were responsible for guiding the incoming troops, ammunition, stores and what have you into the right channels to get forward to the front and that lasted a fair while. The firing went on for two or three days, so we knew it wasn't all over. We knew that the assault troops who'd gone ahead of us were in for a hell of a time. That sense of numbness went. Of course it did. And you then realised what had happened: there were the bodies to prove it. One of your best friends had been killed and you'd lost a couple of men. It wasn't finished by a long way in our minds; you still had the brunt of the war to go through. But D-Day, if it had been unsuccessful, would have meant we'd have lost the war, there's no doubt about that, no doubt at all. But we'd established a beach-head and we'd won the first leg of the game.

GEOFF YOUNG

In 1939 the Wiltshire Regiment came to our village and they were showing off all their new equipment. We were all really impressed and I think thirty-one men joined up that night. Being 17, I was the youngest. I was transferred to the 4th Wiltshire Battalion, which was part of the 43rd Wessex Division, and we landed on Gold Beach on D-Day plus 17. I was told that we were going to

Geoff Young in Germany, 1945. He saw action from D-Day to the end of the war and was Mentioned in Despatches and awarded the Dutch Bronze Cross.

France, that we would be break-out troops and we would cut through the Germans like a knife through butter. But in reality it didn't come off. We didn't realise the extent of the German Army or the fight they were putting up. The 9th and 10th Panzer Divisions had been moved up from Calais and they were in front of us. To combat that was impossible for infantry divisions and our Sherman tanks were out matched all the time.

One of the first things we had to do was to take this hill known as Hill 112. Of all the battles throughout the war, I think that was the most horrendous. It was a hot summer, dry and dusty. I was actually LOB, left out of battle, for the first two days and I was about 500 yards behind the front line. Our company went up into action and unfortunately our artillery fired short and fell on Company HQ and we lost a lot of men. The company commander at the time, Major Ottowell, was very upset about it, as all of us were. Then I was asked to go up to the front because the battalion was moving forward and there were a lot of people not been buried, so I started my war time burying the Dorsets and Hampshires, which was a very sad job. They'd been fighting there six days before and nobody had been up there to do anything about it. I was one of the chaps who started the burying, which I did the best I could, just to get them under the ground because the flies in that heat were very bad. Naturally we left their helmets where they were, so they could have a proper burial later. It was so sad, but

Geoff Young (middle row, second from right) was a keen footballer and is seen here with the 4th Wilts Battalion team.

you're frightened really that it might happen to you. The shelling and mortaring was on then and I thought I might be like one of those chaps before long. This was my first time in action and I was hoping the war would be over before too long, but I think that all of us thought we're not gonna win this war because we couldn't get on to the attack.

I became the jeep driver because the company jeep driver was wounded and he asked me if I could take over. It was then that I became friendly with a chap called Jim Wicks who was the company clerk. He was a 6-foot chap, really jovial, and he was a wonderful poet, a really wonderful chap. He became my trench mate. You used to have two men in a trench and it was always nice to have someone with you. When I was out on the jeep, Jim would start to dig my trench after he'd dug his own: that was the kind of chap he was. It was marvellous to get back and think, 'By golly, he's done it again' because then I could get under cover and that was the main thing. I was most frightened of the artillery and mortar shells, they were landing so close to you and the noise was tremendous. I wasn't worried about machine-gun bullets because if they were gonna hit you, they were gonna hit you and that was it, but I was definitely worried about the shrapnel. That was the most horrendous thing out there.

We eventually went through Hill 112 and then we were told we were to take Mont Pinçon. Major Ottowell was called to a meeting and when he came back he said, 'I'm glad to say that our company is going to lead the 2nd Army up Mont Pinçon', and I thought, 'My golly, what with?' Then he said, 'We're going to lead with the jeep.' This was unorthodox, but we were told to get up as quick as we could. So Major Ottowell came with me in the jeep and at 1800 hours he blew his whistle and off we went. He was stood up in the passenger seat of the jeep with his binoculars, holding his revolver in his right hand. We went about 60 yards and all of a sudden he started shouting, 'Stop, stop, stop. Tiger at 1 o'clock. Back, back, back.' So I backed back about 70 yards to our trenches. Just before we got there, the first shell from the Tiger tank landed about 30 yards away from me and we knew the next shell would hit us. Luckily we'd just got into the trenches when the next shell hit the jeep and up she went. I had ammunition, hand grenades and mortar bombs on board, but fortunately they didn't blow up. The only thing that I was really niggled about was I had a football on the back and it went up in about a thousand pieces! But that was a very scary moment. I was dead lucky. It's providence really, it's the luck of the draw and you just had to hope for the best. But morale was always good and we had to soldier on although we were all frightened.

We then had to go as fast as we could to a place called Vernon, where we were going to make a bridgehead over the River Seine. Again I was told that the jeep would lead the company in. As we got to Vernon all of a sudden crowds were coming out, girls in

Jim Wicks, Geoff Young's friend and trench mate.

The road to Mont Pinçon where Geoff Young was lucky to avoid being hit by a Tiger tank. *(Courtesy of P. Delaforce)*

frocks, and they were shouting and cheering us. It was a great feeling because the French people really did appreciate what we were doing. Then a Resistance man with a Sten gun came out of the crowd and he jumped on the jeep with us and took us down to the river's edge. We went into a house and the family were really excited, they started to get the cognac out, they didn't seem to realise there was a war on. Then the commanders came into the house and they were making all the plans. The 5th Wilts were assigned to go over to the other side and we were instructed to take up positions by the riverside while they crossed. There was smoke being thrown over by the artillery so the Germans couldn't see them coming over, but unfortunately the smoke had blown away and when the 5th Wilts got halfway, they got stuck on the sand banks and they were mown down. It was one of the most horrific times and I thought, 'What on Earth are we doing?' If we could have just taken our time a bit and made sure about it. The 5th Wilts lost 120 men dead within about 20 minutes and we couldn't do anything about it. Eventually the Royal Engineers put a bridge across and I came over the bridge.

Above: British troops lie along the banks of the River Seine, giving covering fire to those crossing. The 5th Battalion of the Wiltshire Regiment saw heavy casualties here. *(IWM BU65)*

Below: Eventually Geoff Young crossed by bridge. *(IWMBU36348)*

Later, we were in Belgium on 24 hours standby waiting for Operation Market Garden to start and on 17 September it started. In the afternoon a despatch rider came up from battalion HQ and he had orders that we had to send a recce jeep with three sergeants right to the front to Lieutenant-Colonel 'Joe' Vandeleur who was with the 3rd Irish Guards leading the attack. The despatch rider said, 'You're for it again, Geoff.' So off we went, with the three sergeants and the company second-in-command, Captain Gilson. I had to pass a column of Sherman tanks, half-tracks, all sorts of vehicles that were going forward in one long line. All of a sudden we came to a violent stop, there were these almighty bangs and nine tanks of the Irish Guards were blown up. I was 300 yards behind those tanks.

Everybody was shouting, 'Keep to the centre of the road! It's mines!' So Captain Gilson went to the front of the line to see what was happening and when he came back he said that it wasn't mines it was a Panzerfaust, which was a German anti-tank weapon. So he ordered the three sergeants who were on the jeep into the woods where the firing had come from and they brought back three German prisoners who gave themselves up. But because the tanks had all brewed up, it was 20 or 30 minutes before we could move the column on.

That was our first obstruction in Market Garden and from then on it was always obstructions, and that's why we couldn't get to the Airborne. We carried on and

Geoff Young in Holland in 1945.

crossed a number of bridges until eventually we arrived in Nijmegen at ten-to-eleven at night on 20 September. I moved the jeep into this garden recess and Captain Gilson went off to wait for the rest of the battalion. He'd been gone so long that it was about 6 o'clock in the morning when five German paratroopers came over the wall. It took me by surprise and it frightened me but I got the Sten gun and I put it on the stretcher frame and got a good aim. I thought, 'Well, if they're gonna come to me, I've gotta dispatch them. I probably can't do the whole lot, but I'll do the best I can.' Then all of a sudden they stopped and they started walking back, away from me and I felt very relieved. I hadn't shot anybody by that time and Sten guns were known to misfire. I didn't want to be a big hero, so that let me off the hook!

Captain Gilson and some officers came back about 11.20 the next morning and told me we had 10 minutes to get to Nijmegen Bridge to rendezvous with the battalion commander and the adjutant. So we got in my jeep and drove until we came across an Irish Guards half-track with one Guard standing there.

A German soldier lies dead on Nijmegen Bridge. Geoff Young miraculously survived after being shot in the head by a German officer nearby. *(IWM EA51313)*

He said that his officers were about 75 yards further along, so my officers went up to see them and I stayed by the half-track with this Guard. We were just about to have a discussion when he shouted out, 'Look out, Jerry officer behind you.' And before I could do anything, I was shot in the back of the head. Luckily for me it was only a small calibre revolver that German officers used to carry. For 2 minutes I didn't know whether I was coming or going. I didn't know whether to cry, laugh, anything and I thought, 'This is the end for me.' I've never felt anything like it in all my life. It was a terrible pain in my head. I've had that pain very occasionally ever since and the bullet's still there.

It stunned me, naturally, and then this Irish Guardsman came towards me and a shell landed behind him, threw him into me and we both fell down an incline. I thought I was badly wounded because I was caught by the blast and I thought I was bleeding, but it was my water bottle had been destroyed and water was going down my leg. I was a bit dazed but I picked the Guardsman up, dragged him up the bank and put him in the jeep passenger seat. How I got him in there I don't know. A medical officer and two stretcher-bearers came up and looked at him and said, 'I'm sorry, soldier, the Guardsman's dead,' so that shook me really. Then they stripped me down to the waist and gave me a good check over. He said, 'I'm sorry, soldier, but it's not a Blighty for you.' But I didn't mind because I still wanted to be with my friends and I was looking forward to getting to Germany.

After I got wounded I was sent back to HQ in Nijmegen to recover. Then we moved on to a place called Drill and had to take up positions there. We entrenched ourselves round a farmstead and my job then was drive the jeep backwards and forwards to battalion HQ, which was about a mile away, to pick up tea, rations and ammunition. On the third day I went up my friend Jim Wicks said, 'I'm gonna say goodbye, Geoff. I'm sorry you've got to go.' So I shook his hand and said, 'Good luck, Jim.' The next morning the Germans put in an attack and Jim was badly wounded. The adjutant came up to me and said, 'Young, I've got a message from your company to say that your friend Jim Wicks is in a gully, map reference so and so, with two stretcher-bearers. They're unable to move and machine guns are keeping them down.' I had to go out for him; there were no two ways about it. So I went to see the regimental first aid post sergeant and I said to him, 'Could you tell me about the Geneva Convention? If I put a Red Cross flag up and I've got ammunition on the jeep, would that be allowed?' He said, 'Oh, I should take a chance.' So I put the Red Cross flag up, hoping that the Germans would take notice of it, and I set off. A burst of machine-gun fire came across the front of me and then they must have

THE GLORIOUS P.B.I.

They wear just common battle dress,
   I wonder if that's why,
They're often termed and sometimes spurned
   As the common P.B.I.

The dust of France clings in their throats,
   Their tongues are cracked and dry,
They don't complain in wind and rain,
   These hardened P.B.I.

They're not the heroes of the sky,
   Nor of the blazing sun,
But on the land they're doing grand,
   The fighting P.B.I.

o-o-o-o-o-o-o-o-o

There's miles and miles of soil to free,
   There'll be lots of things to try,
Those sweating men, those dusty men,
   Of the wonderful P.B.I.

Our dearest friends they saw us off,
   'Twas hard to say goodbye,
But we left the shores to settle scores,
   The new born P.B.I.

Remember then those marching men,
   With God, you can rely,
To thrash the hun and when it's done,
   To thank the P.B.I.

We know how you will welcome us,
   On you our future lie,
We'll try our best to do our best,
   The home-sick P.B.I.

You'll find us strange when we return,
   You'll have to soothe and try,
To do your best with lots of rest,
   To the tired P.B.I.

And when the war's been fought and won,
   Pray for those who lie,
Drowned in the surf or neath French turf,
   Those valiant P.B.I.

And when the last "All Clear" has gone,
   You'll lift your hearts and cry,
"O thank the Lord, and praise the sword
   Of the glorious P.B.I."

o-o-o-o-o-o-o-o-o

'The Glorious PBI (Poor Bloody Infantry)' – a poem by Jim Wicks that sums up the lot of an infantryman.

seen the flag and they stopped. When I got to the gully the two stretcher-bearers were there and Jim said, 'I knew you'd come for me, Geoff.' I thought, 'He's not so badly wounded', but they'd given him morphine so he was a bit dopey really. He said, 'I've got it in the midriff.' So I said, 'All right Jim, I'll get you back as soon as I can.'

The stretcher-bearers put him on the jeep and clamped him on the stretcher frame and we drove off. All of a sudden there was an almighty rumble and a tremendous amount of heavy artillery came down. It was so heavy I couldn't go into it. It was impossible, so I pulled into a bungalow where there was an anti-tank gun with a crew. I had some mail on the jeep and I sorted the mail out for Jim. He'd had three letters from home that day and he read his letters. We were there about 10 minutes and then we went back to HQ. There was an ambulance waiting for Jim and he was taken back to Eindhoven. They put him on a plane but apparently he died before the plane took off. They said he'd died of shock. He was buried in a cemetery near Eindhoven. The company commander told me and I couldn't believe it. In actual fact it was the first time that tears came to my eyes. I couldn't speak and I was quite numb. I couldn't face the company commander and I had to turn away. It took me quite a while to get over it. We did miss him very much indeed, but that friendship has lasted 60 years because I've been out to his grave lots of times. I promised him, in my thoughts, that I would go and to visit him.

Going up into Germany, in the Rhineland on the way to Goch, we came to a little village. We'd already taken our positions up that day, on the left-hand side of A Company, and we got an urgent message to say, 'Could you send your jeep over to help us out, we're in dire trouble. We're being attacked heavily and we've got lots of casualties.' I drove to A Company and I went to see Sergeant-Major Oram in the village hall, who was in charge of the company at the time. He told me where the casualties were – they were up through some houses. The mortaring and shelling was so heavy that I couldn't go out. Then all of a sudden the mortaring hit the roof off the village hall, so I thought I might as well go.

There was a house with like a helter-skelter outside and there was a German paratrooper coming down there. He was slightly wounded and he had his Schmeisser light machine gun wrapped round his neck. He took me by surprise and I took him by surprise. He said, 'Kamerad, kamerad,' so I beckoned him towards me and all of a sudden, two shots rang out and he fell down. There were two British chaps on the side of me and I said, 'Bloody hell, you've shot a prisoner.' I went to him and I had plenty of field dressings on me, so I put two field dressings in his stomach to ease his pain and try to stop the bleeding. As I

Margrit Young at the age of 16. Her family were lucky to escape the Allied bombing of Hanover in 1943.

was kneeling down to him he touched my hand, he didn't have the strength to hold it, he touched my hand and he said, 'Tommy, Danke schon, for you, the Iron Cross.' And I thought that was the best thing I heard during the war. It was marvellous to think that an enemy soldier had appreciated what I tried to do for him. It was fantastic to hear that. All of a sudden, as I was knelt down, I had a Tommy gun pushed in the back of my neck and this British soldier said, 'If you bloody well help him, you're a dead man.' I couldn't believe this was happening. Fortunately, Captain Hamilton came up and said, 'What's this all about?' and they ran off. I said to Captain Hamilton, 'What are his chances, sir?' and he said, 'Not much I'm afraid.' They took him away and I didn't know what happened to him.

About four days before the end of the war I took a recce party into a small village. We went to see the Burgomeister to ask him if we could take over about three or four houses for our company to move into. But the Burgomeister couldn't speak English, so he said he'd go and get a young lady who could. The girl's name was Margrit. She was very attractive and spoke very good English, and it didn't matter that she was German. I didn't have any animosity towards the Germans at all. They were good fighters and I appreciated that and respected them. She had been bombed out of Hanover in the fire bombing in November 1943 and they were lucky to have escaped with their lives. For a fortnight I used to take her around on the jeep and she used to help with things. She even helped us find a football pitch! Unfortunately we were moved to another village, but I was able see her occasionally, about once a fortnight.

The memorial to the 43rd Wessex Division which stands at the top of Hill 112. *(Courtesy of P. Delaforce)*

When it came to the time I was going to be demobbed I thought, 'I'm not going to see this girl again and I've got so used to her, I wonder if this is the right girl for me?' So I said to her, 'Do you mind if we correspond?' When I got back to England we corresponded and eventually she came over to England. On 17 May 1947 we got married.

The 43rd Wessex Division meant a lot to me because I was with them for three and a half years. I was very proud to serve with them and especially the 4th Battalion of the Wiltshire Regiment. To me they were like a band of brothers.

SIX

HELL IN THE JUNGLE

Our Boys in Burma

When the Japanese bombed the United States Pacific Fleet at Pearl Harbor on 7 December 1941 it signalled their entry into a war with the West that would last for almost four years. Within two months Britain's fortress Singapore was in Japanese hands and over 130,000 Allied troops had been transported into captivity. Many thousands would not survive to see the end of the war. In Burma British troops, including the 1st Battalion of the Glosters, fought a desperate rearguard action as

Major General William Slim. *(IWM SE3310)*

the Japanese Army forced them to retreat north towards India and by May 1942 they had completed the longest withdrawal in the history of the British Army. But the Japanese had not counted on the skill and determination of Major General William Slim, Commander of Allied troops in Burma. Slim was born near Bristol in 1897 and had been wounded at Gallipoli during the First World War. In the months and years that were to follow, he proved himself a truly great commander and by the time he led Allied troops back into Rangoon in the summer of 1945, he had become the only British general of the Second World War to have fought against the same enemy throughout a campaign in which defeat had been turned into victory.

The turning point in the war in Burma began in 1944 with the successful Allied defence of Kohima and Imphal, which prevented the Japanese from gaining ground in Assam. These battles raged from March until June at a cost of some 4,000 British troops and were finally brought to an end through a brilliantly executed plan, devised and implemented by ex-Clifton College pupil Derek Horsford, who at the time was a 27-year-old lieutenant-colonel commanding the 4th/1st Gurkhas. His plan was later used as a model of its kind and won Lieutenant-Colonel

Fierce fighting took place across a mined tennis court at Kohima. *(IWM IND3483)*

Chindits lay explosives on a railway line. *(IWM SE7921)*

Horsford his first Distinguished Service Order. He would later become Major-General Brigade of Gurkhas.

From Kohima and Imphal, Allied forces began the long push back towards Rangoon, aided by the guerrilla tactics of the Chindits, the newly formed special service forces who operated deep behind enemy lines, disrupting transport and communication lines with increasing success. But this was a long and bitter struggle for regular soldiers like Dennis Greenslade, made all the worse by the unforgiving terrain and fanatical opposition. Front-line troops relied exclusively on air drops for food and supplies and diseases like malaria were rife. But still morale was kept high by the fact that the Allies continued to move forward.

Meanwhile, in prisoner-of-war camps around the Far East British captives were struggling to stay alive at the hands of their tormentors. Starvation, disease and ritual punishment became a part of everyday life and many died during the extreme hardships of forced labour. Ted Davis had been captured when the Japanese routed the Dutch East Indies and was held for three and a half years in Borneo. By the time he was finally released in 1945, he weighed just 6½ stone.

On 3 May 1945 Allied forces finally reached the Burmese capital of Rangoon, but it would take until August and the dropping of the atomic

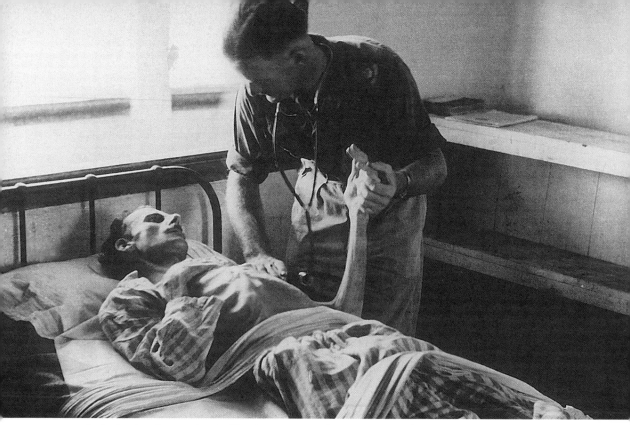

A doctor treats a seriously ill prisoner at Kuching prisoner-of-war camp after liberation. *(IWM HU42495)*

bombs on Hiroshima and Nagasaki for the Japanese to surrender, finally bringing to an end the war in the Far East. Many of those who fought through the Burma campaign considered themselves to be part of a forgotten army. Ted Davis and many like him found it difficult to adjust to life out of captivity and others missed the comradeship that life in the jungle had offered them. But they had survived one of the most brutal campaigns of the war and today they wear their Burma Star with pride.

It should also be remembered that the war in the Far East was truly an international conflict and Britain remains indebted to her Commonwealth allies who fought and died alongside her own men.

DEREK HORSFORD

My father was in the British Army, and my mother had relatives in the Indian Army. At the time you got double pay for joining the Indian Army, so that's what I decided to do! When you joined the Indian Army, you spent your first year with a British regiment in India as a platoon commander, where you learnt all the basic things like weapons training and courts martial and things like

Derek Horsford (centre of middle row, wearing white jacket) was a pupil at Clifton College in Bristol. He is seen here with the college cricket team.

that, and I joined the Cameronians. During that time you learnt the language of the regiment you were going to and in my case, as I was going to the Gurkhas, I learnt Gurkhali. You had to pass first of all your Urdu, which was the language of India, and then I joined the 1st/8th Gurkhas in Pakistan as Company Commander. When you first join the Gurkhas, they're not all that friendly to you until they get to know you, but you've got to prove yourself. So it was quite a lot of responsibility for a chap of 21, commanding about 100 men. But they did respect the British officer if he was good and if he could talk their language. Their discipline was so wonderful and they had a great sense of humour.

We trained for the North-West Frontier. We then moved up to the frontier and used to go out two or three times a week on what we called road protection, opening the road, picketing the heights and being shot at. But it was a wonderful life; we worked hard and we played hard and we were terribly fit. I think one of the highlights for me up there was being sent up to Alexandra Piquet, which was the highest piquet in the British Empire, at about 8,000 feet, and it commanded a very extensive area of hills. It was manned by about fifty Gurkhas and I was in charge of them for about a fortnight. It was a very exciting thing to see the Union Jack flying over this piquet and realising I was

in charge. There was a tremendous sense of pride in the British Empire and
when I was at school the whole map was painted red. Here was I, aged 21,
defending the most important part of the British Empire. I suppose it does seem
extraordinary now, but every night one had to change into blue patrols and sit
down to dinner, all by myself, and be waited on by Gurkha waiters.

Of course we were worried about the Japanese getting into India and we
moved down on my birthday to the Arakan in Burma to fight the Japs down
there. I was sent by my commanding officer up into the Mayu Range, which is
the range of hills running north and south dividing the Arakan. I was sent up
there to stop the Japs coming over from east to west. I had about 200 men with
me and I used to send out patrols every night. In the morning I used to get their
reports, then I'd report down to the plains, to the brigadier, saying we'd killed
so many Japs last night and two Japs the night before that and five Japs the
night before that and so on. He sent me up a message saying he didn't believe
me. He thought I was exaggerating and he wanted some proof, so I briefed the
Gurkha patrol the next day and I said, 'Bring back the heads.' Into my dugout
at about 6 o'clock in the morning came three heads. They'd bored a hole in the
skulls, put some jungle twine through and knotted it, so these heads bounced
on the end of this twine. We put them in a sack and I said to one of the

Derek Horsford, second from right, 1938.

Gurkhas, 'Go into the brigadier's tent, stand to attention, salute him and upend the sack,' which he did. I gather the brigade commander was nearly sick and he sent me up a message saying, 'Never do that again. In future I'll believe you!'

The Japanese soldiers were very good soldiers, very brave. Once the officers had made a plan they wouldn't change it, so the Japanese soldiers had to go on and on and on until they got their objective. We used to say that the most efficient army in the world would be Japanese soldiers officered by British officers. Oh, they were good and we had great respect for them.

I was second-in-command, but I was LOB, left out of battle. You had various officers left out of battle in case people got killed, to relieve them, and I was left out of battle in case my commanding officer got wounded or killed. But I was bored stiff because I wasn't allowed to go forward, so I got myself attached to Brigade Headquarters as a duty officer. And I was on duty one night when suddenly a signal came in saying the corps commander, who was a lieutenant-general, wished to see me at 10 o'clock the following morning. Well, I was absolutely scared stiff. Why would a very senior general want to see me, a major? I put on my best jungle green, got into the jeep and motored up to Corps Headquarters where I was met by the general's ADC who had a smile on his face, which I thought was a good sign. I was ushered into the general's tent.

A general view of the terrain at Kohima, showing the ridges and peaks that dominate the landscape. *(IWM IND3410)*

He stood up and smiled and held out his hand, another good sign, and he then said, 'Horsford, sit down please.' Then he came up with this bombshell: 'I want you to fly up to Calcutta tonight in an aeroplane, get yourself outfitted as a 1st Gurkha, then get up to Kohima within two days and take command of the 4th Battalion of the 1st Gurkhas who are in operation against the Japs in Kohima.'

I was a major, but I was about to become a lieutenant-colonel, so the first thing I did was put up lieutenant-colonel's badges of rank because lieutenant-colonels were honorary members of the very exclusive Bengal Club in Calcutta. So I spent two nights sleeping between sheets, having jolly good food. Then I got into a train in Calcutta, with a bottle of whisky, and I think I stayed up most of the night sipping whisky and saying to myself, 'What the hell do I do? Here am I, about to command a new battalion, I don't know anybody in it and we're fighting the Japs.' But you just took it in your stride, quite honestly. We were training for it. One had read a lot of books about how to beat the Japanese and we trained the Gurkhas how to do it. Eventually I arrived and the first thing I was told was that the brigade commander wanted to see me. He would be my immediate boss. So I said, 'Where is he?' and they said, 'Up there, on that hill.' So I went up and there were machine guns firing at him, bullets flying around the place, shells landing and there he was, as if nothing was going on! I stayed flat on my face, and he said, 'You're new here, so I won't commit you to battle for a week so that you get to know your British officers and your Gurkha officers.' But two days later he committed to a battalion night attack against the Japs! Luckily, that was a fairly simple one because most of the Japs had gone.

Anyhow, then I got on to this place called the Treasury and from there you can see this huge great ridge known as the Naga Village, which overlooked the whole of Kohima, so I had a wonderful view of that. I saw a battalion going along a knife edge to attack the Japanese, who had strongpoints on that knife edge, but the battalion was absolutely decimated and had to withdraw. A couple of days later another battalion went in along this knife edge and they were decimated. I remember saying to my officers, 'The brigade commander is now going to send for me and tell me to have a go and I'm going to refuse.' I'd had time to work out a plan of taking the whole battalion by night, right round behind the Japs. I'd had about ten days to think about it and I'd sent Gurkha patrols out into the Jap positions to tell me if certain hills were held and if so,

Opposite: A Gurkha soldier hides in undergrowth. Their daring night reconnaissance helped Derek Horsford to devise his plan. *(IWM IB229)*

by how many people. Imagine what that must have been like – in the dark, in the jungle, creeping along very close to the Japs, but the Gurkhas were terribly brave. Anyway, following these patrols I had this wonderful picture of these hills: two were not being held but the third one was. So when the brigade commander sent for me, and was about to tell me to tack along this ridge I said, 'I've got another plan, sir,' and he listened to it. As I drove off in the jeep he threw his fist at me and he said, 'It bloody well better work or I'll sack you.'

By night we got two companies on to the hills behind the Japs and I sent a third company up to attack the hill which was occupied, by which time we had guns and tanks and aircraft supporting us. I think the exciting part about that was I made the Gurkhas wear white towels on their backs so that I could see them and tell the tanks not to fire at them. We sat in a trench on a hill, quite a long way away, waiting for the attack to happen, when suddenly a cloud burst came down and I couldn't see any white towels at all. I thought the Gurkhas were late starting their attack, so I told the guns and the tanks to stop firing. After 5 minutes the cloud cleared and the tanks started firing again. But the Gurkhas weren't late: they were on time, but they took no notice of the fact that guns were firing and shells were landing just in front of them and they got to this hill where the Japs were and found them crouching in their trenches, terrified of being shot up. I think we killed about twenty of them in their trenches. Then all hell was let loose and we were shelled, mortared and machine gunned. The general said to me on the radio, 'For God's sake stay there and don't leave that position for two days.' It was hell and you couldn't lift your head up to have a look without being shot at.

So we were there for two very, very uncomfortable days. But we were on the objective. We hadn't got the final hill, Hunter's Hill, which was a bit further on. The general told me not to bother, that he'd send another battalion to do that, but I wanted to get that last hill! I was being shot at the whole time, so I got into a tank and we went up fairly close so that I could see the hill through the tank periscope. Then I told the tank commander to go back; he backed into a shell hole and the whole tank disappeared with me in it. The Gurkhas roared with laughter at that. But just before I was relieved one of my company commanders said, 'I think I can do it, I don't think there are any Japs there.' So he rushed up the hill, about 100 yards, and he got this last hill. We then came back to rest and I remember

going round all the tents that night, drinking rum with the Gurkhas in each tent and congratulating them and singing Gurkha songs with them. I think it took me all night long, but you knew then that you'd got them absolutely behind you.

After Kohima, the Japanese retreat started and of course we followed them up after that, all the way down through Burma. It was a long way from Kohima down to Rangoon and we were fighting virtually the whole way. The Japs were retreating but they were holding us up with little pockets of resistance everywhere – and pretty big pockets sometimes. It was just going flat out the whole way, attacking hills, attacking jungle, attacking the oil fields and we didn't get much rest. But it was quite exciting because they were on the run.

I'd started training the battalion for jungle warfare on the North-West Frontier where there were no trees, so we used to have jungle exercises without trees! When we went into the jungle in Burma I think most of us felt quite safe because you could hide in the jungle. We used to say, 'Those poor chaps in the desert, in the 8th Army, they have nowhere to hide.' We felt much safer in the jungle. There was a very nasty time once when we came upon a small copse and there were about a dozen Gurkhas tied to trees. They'd been slit right down the middle by the Japanese. They were cut in two and that really infuriated us. We really thought, 'Right, if we see a Jap again, there's no mercy.' That was horrible. But I never worried that I wouldn't get through. I was 27 and my British officers were younger than me, except for one or two, and most of us weren't married, so the whole thing was exciting. We longed for the war to end, towards the end, but you didn't really visualise life at home. The only thing that

Devastation at Kohima Ridge after the fighting. *(IWM IND3697)*

Gurkhas march into Rangoon.

occurred to us was that we were going to beat these bloody Japs. We were on the advance in '44 and '45, so our morale was very high and we had very few casualties because one thing I was absolutely adamant about was that we would never undertake an operation where I knew we would have a lot of casualties.

I can remember the end of the war very well because I was in the Bengal Club in Calcutta thoroughly enjoying myself when I heard on the radio that we had dropped the atomic bomb on Japan. Then I came home to England. It was lovely seeing my parents again. My brother was a Gurkha too and I sometimes now wonder what my parents must have gone through with their only two sons fighting the Japs in Burma, but we both came through all right.

Not only was it a great honour to command the Gurkhas, but it was wonderful to command them. They were wonderful chaps, very brave and bloody good soldiers. I remember before the attack at Kohima one of our positions was shelled and I was told a Gurkha had been very badly wounded so I went up to see him. He was lying there and the whole of his stomach was lying open because he had been hit by a shell. It was the rainy season and he was shovelling mud into his stomach. I asked the doctor who was nearby, 'Will, he live?' and he said, 'No, no chance at all.' So I told the doctor to give him an overdose of morphine, because I didn't want to see him in terrible pain, which

Derek Horsford later became Major General Brigade of Gurkhas. His strategy helped change Allied fortunes at Kohima and has become a model of its kind.

the doctor did. About six months later I got a letter from this Gurkha, from Nepal, thanking me for saving his life!

Later, when I ended up as Major General Brigade of Gurkhas I used to go up to Nepal to watch the soldiers come down to be recruited. Their first choice was the British Army, their second choice was the Indian Army and their third choice was the Nepalese Army. I can't remember the figures but we used to take hundreds a year in the old days. In my day they were only taking about 400 a year and thousands had to go back to their villages in tears.

DENNIS GREENSLADE

Early in the war I was working for the Ministry of Supply as a timber feller, cutting down pit props for the mines. We worked very long hours and nobody seemed to appreciate what we were doing, so I thought I would follow my father, who had volunteered in the '14–18 war, so I volunteered for service as soon as I was old enough, in 1942. I went to Bradford for six weeks' elementary training and then they posted me to the South Wales Borderers. I'd never even been to Wales or knew anything about it, really. We ended up at Ryde in

Dennis Greenslade followed his father into the Army.

Sussex, doing invasion repelling exercises. They moved us around quite a lot. Early in 1944, when D-Day was imminent, we were split up and I went to the depot at Brecon and from there I went to the Far East. They just selected 3,000 people from the training camp and we were put on a boat at Liverpool. We ended up in Bombay for the Burma campaign.

From Bombay we went across by train to the Central Provinces: five days and five nights on the train, not very far actually, it was only about 1,000 miles or so, but they were slow trains. It was quite an adventure until we got to the front line because it was exciting and you saw something new every day. After our training there we were sent on a boat on the Brahmaputra River. We spent about 12 hours on the boat, a two-deck thing, and then we were flown into an airfield north of Mandalay. There were shells bursting, grenades, rifle fire, machine gun fire, all the terrible things that are associated with war, and we were in single file, creeping through the jungle undergrowth towards the front line. Suddenly I saw two people coming back on stretchers, both of whom had travelled out with me to India on the boat. If you wanted anything to frighten you that was one of them, one of the things that put the fear of hell into you, to see colleagues already wounded and they hadn't even arrived at the front line.

When we got to the front line, we found that conditions were horrendous; the horrors, the hardships and deprivation were beyond the scope of the imagination of most people. The conditions were terrible; going without food, wet through in the monsoon all the time, no change of clothing. Then scalding heat when

British troops make their way carefully through long grass, always on the look-out for Japanese snipers. *(IWM IND3479)*

the rain stopped and the sun came through and the temperature can be up to 120 in the shade, quite dreadful. Prior to the rain arriving, the monsoon proper, you get tremendous lightning, thunder and vibrations of the earth, so much so that I really thought something serious was going to happen. People who had gone through a monsoon before told me it was normal. Of course, when the rain started, it was stair-rod rain, and it goes on for days. The next morning, after the rain, the bridges are all washed away by the rush of the water.

We joined up with the 2nd Welch Regiment and they were in the 19th Indian Division. They were going down through the centre of Burma and I was posted into C Company. By that time the 2nd Welch were down to about 300 men from about 800, so they were desperate for people. One of the first tasks we were given was to cut off the road between Lashio and Mandalay, where all the Japanese reinforcements were being channelled. We used to lie low during the day and creep through the undergrowth, missing the rivers, by night. Finally, we arrived at the foot of this steep climb of about 4,500 feet and when we got to the top, we moved about 6 miles towards Mandalay and set up an ambush. The Japanese High Command had ordered their troops to hold Mandalay at all costs and to hold us behind the mighty Irrawaddy River, because if they couldn't stop

Like many Allied soldiers, Dennis Greenslade (left) was worried about being captured.

the British at that river, which was a minimum of 1¼ miles wide, they weren't going to be able to stop us anywhere.

Later that day, it must have been 8 o'clock in the evening – but time doesn't mean anything in these circumstances, except dark and light – along came a Japanese convoy. We had Mark IV Lee Enfield rifles and Bren guns and of course we shot up the first vehicles and the last vehicles and cut off their route. It wasn't a very nice experience. There's a lot of fear and you're frightened to death to start with, but you realise it's them or you. I always thought if I was shooting at someone that he must have parents and he must have relatives and I didn't like the idea, but it was him or me. We captured thirty-six 3-ton lorries, a jeep and masses of booty in that ambush. There was a lot of blood, but no Japanese, so they must have escaped into the jungle.

We soon saw the brutality of the Japanese. They were barbaric. We used to call them 'terrorists in uniform' because that's what they were. It's strange: after the initial few days I wasn't worried about being killed, but I was really concerned about being wounded and captured because they had a habit of tying our wounded to a tree, leaving them overnight and using them for bayonet practice the next day. On another occasion a couple of our chaps had their private parts cut away when they were captured and I can only imagine the horrors and the pain that went with bleeding to death under those circumstances. So if they captured someone, that person was lucky if they got a bullet between the eyes, and that happened sometimes in the jungle. I caught a Japanese prisoner once, a young lad, and although I couldn't converse with him I treated him well because I thought that there weren't many Japanese who gave themselves up, it wasn't one of the things they would do normally. My colleagues thought I was being too kind to him, but in fact it worked to our advantage because they took him back for interrogation and he was able to give us a lot of help, so I felt good about that. I wish I'd taken his name so I could have contacted him after the war.

The Japanese used smaller calibre ammunition than us, on the basis that a wounded man was more problem than a dead one. Often they tied their snipers in the tops of trees, so we had to bring them down or kill them because if they shot one of our chaps, the leading scout for example, and you sent someone to pick him up, the sniper would get that person as well. We had all sorts of problems with snipers, but it made you very aware of your surroundings. I was never so aware of my surroundings as I was in the jungle fighting the Japanese. I was brought up carrying a shotgun from the age of 11, so in the jungle I was asked to deal with the snipers because they knew that I was accurate with a rifle. There was no problem with it, once you could find the right position. It was a necessary thing to do and we were trained to do it, to be able to kill.

But we were often near the Japanese in the jungle. For instance we used to make harbour at 5 o'clock in the evening when we were advancing. We dug ourselves into the ground, then we'd throw a cordon of wire with some tins on around us, so that if anybody came through they would rattle the tins. Then the Japanese would come round and we had what we called jitter attacks and they used to call out, 'We're coming to get you, Johnny.' They weren't very far away, only a matter of yards, and they would throw stones or grenades. That was quite frightening.

Following spread: Mortaring was often the best way to make progress in the jungle. *(IWM IND 4723)*

On the road to Mandalay. After the success at Kohima, British troops continued to advance through Burma. *(IWM IND4488)*

There's nothing like problems for welding people together. It's problems that really pull people together and give you camaraderie. In the jungle, you just built up a kind of friendship that you couldn't possibly have under any other circumstances. It's difficult to describe. You valued their presence and they valued yours. It was a real camaraderie, but it had to be, it couldn't afford to be any other way. I had a great friend called Jake Waters from Newport in South Wales. His people were tanners. He was in the 2nd Welch with me. A number of our people were going to cross a chaung, which is a fast-flowing stream in the monsoon season, and this one was about 75 yards wide. We had home-made rafts and about six went on one particular raft and they were washed away, including Jake. I saw him washed away and I never saw him again. I felt terrible about it, but there was nothing I could do. You became so hardened to it, it's strange. Sometimes a mosquito bite was more harmful to you than hearing the shells going overhead.

In the jungle you have to turn to something for comfort and I found much comfort from praying. I was brought up strictly in the Church of England religion and my parents insisted that I attended church at least once on a Sunday. So in the jungle I just prayed that I'd be safe, that I'd pull through, because it was a terrible time. I don't think there were any atheists in the front line, quite honestly. Everybody prayed, I'm sure they did. When you could hear the shells coming over, that was a time for prayer. Was that shell going to land on you and kill you or not? I had a couple of lucky escapes from shelling. One night I was in a trench with a young chap and when daylight came he was lying down as though he was asleep, but in fact he'd been killed by a blast from a shell and I survived. On another occasion, at Mandalay, I was with a chap called Harold Puddy and we were trying to get into Fort Dufferin to get the Japs out. There's was a thick wall, about 32 feet thick, and up to 30 feet high and we couldn't get in. The major-general asked for air support and the Americans tried to bomb the fort. But they did so from such a high altitude that they missed. The chap that was standing next to me received a piece of shrapnel in his side and he carried it with him for a long time, but we could easily have been killed there. That was a lucky escape for me, but only the lucky ones came back, of course, didn't they?

We relied completely on air drops for our food. When there was going to be an air drop we had to make a clearing and the planes would drop supplies. If it was food, it would be dropped by free fall from about 50 or 60 feet above the

Aerial bombing at Fort Dufferin, where Dennis Greenslade was lucky to escape injury. *(IWM SE3474)*

tree line. If it was ammunition or radio equipment, it would be dropped by parachute from about 600 to 800 feet. But we never got proper food. The food supplies that came by air were just water biscuits and things that we're not used to eating. We never had any meat or green vegetables. The Japanese had learnt how to eat snakes and the roots from certain plants, but we didn't have the training for that, so we had to go hungry. We did eat raw pineapples that we found growing, but I didn't eat anything else like that because you couldn't risk it. On one occasion we had an air drop of Indian food. Now I never thought I would eat Indian food, the curries and spices and things, but I did. Later, we fought alongside the Gurkhas and I got used to sharing Indian food with them.

Of course, if you found anything that was left behind by the Japanese, the chances are it would have been poisoned and they used to poison the wells as well. The water we had to drink was like brown gravy and we had a treatment to put in it to make it safe because the rivers would have had dead bodies floating in them, dead animals, you can't imagine. But you can't live very long in the Burma jungle without water because

Air drops in the jungle were crucial to Allied success. (IWM CB135851)

you're perspiring profusely all the time and you lose a lot of weight. I lost about 2 stone, but that was all right. One of the biggest problems was tiredness because we would be on the front line for five days, sometimes six, without sleep. I learnt to sleep standing up, like an elephant or a horse. You couldn't afford to go to sleep and you weren't allowed to go to sleep because you might well be surrounded by Japanese, who could attack at any time. Part of the reason for tiredness was hunger, of course, but you've got to bear in mind that we were extremely fit people when we first went into the jungle. Had we not been, we would not have survived.

Memories of war in the jungle returned to haunt Dennis Greenslade (standing, middle) for many years.

Towards the end I was suffering from jungle sores, I had a lot of jungle sores on me. When I went into hospital, the nurse looked at some of the sores on my shinbone and she said, 'These things don't heal out here. You'll probably have to go back to England.' So I said, quite quickly, 'How soon?' But in the event, they sent me up into the hills, at 6,000 feet at Assam in India. The climate there is much different to what it is down on the plains so the sores healed, but I still get trouble from them now. We were supposed to take an anti-malaria treatment everyday and we were threatened with court martial if we came down with it. But it didn't work and after I was hospitalised I got malaria, so I was in hospital shortly before the end of the war.

When I came out, I travelled back to the forward reinforcement camp. I read the orders and I saw that my name was down to go back in the front line the next day and I thought that was strange because some of the troops at the camp had been there for nine months without going to the front. So I went to the corporal clerk and asked him why I was on draft when other people hadn't been near the front line and he said, 'Yes, but they haven't got any battle experience.' I was really annoyed and I said, 'I don't expect you have either,' and stomped out of the tent, thinking he'd put me on a charge. In the event, that was the day the first atom bomb was dropped and everything stopped. Of course it was a tremendous relief. You can't explain the relief that the war was over and that we would be going home some time.

But strangely enough I was always optimistic about us winning the war. We were always going forward and I thought we were bound to win if we kept going forward. I've got a copy of a letter at home that I wrote home to my parents in which I said things that were very optimistic, which surprises me now when I read it, having regard to the conditions we were under. But I've never forgotten about my time in the jungle. When I first got married, my wife used to tell me that I'd woken up in the night screaming. That went on for years and years and even today I occasionally dream about my experiences in Burma.

TED DAVIS

I was born in Bath and I was called up in 1940. I was in the RAOC, the Ordnance Corps, and in 1942 I was posted to Egypt and worked recovering tanks in the Western Desert. I was posted to the Far East in 1942 with B Squadron of the Royal Hussars and I didn't like the idea of going out to fight the Japanese. We were designated as the first batch of light tanks for India, but

Ted Davis in 1941.

we ended up going to Sumatra. Then we evacuated Sumatra and crossed into Java. When the Japanese landed in Java, all we could do was retreat. The Dutch were the colonial power on Java and there were a few Dutch troops there, but mostly their army was Javanese people. But when the Japanese landed, the Javanese people just discarded their uniforms and faded away, so there was no real army there at all. Our squadron leader went off to consult the Dutch people in command and he came back and told us that they had capitulated. It was every man for himself, so three of us decided to take our weapons and try to get to a port on the other side of the island, where there might be a boat. It was on that trip that we first ran into the Japanese and encountered their brutality. We spoke to this Japanese soldier and before you knew where you were he just hit you around the head and we didn't know why. We later learned that every time you approached a Japanese soldier, you had to bow. If you didn't bow, you got a walloping. We felt bloody humiliated, but you had to do it or suffer a beating up. I was then transported to Singapore by the Japanese and then to Sarawak, Borneo, which became our permanent prison camp.

The message my mother got from the War Office was that I was a prisoner of war of the Japanese. That's how it was regarded in this country. But the Japanese didn't regard us as prisoners of war. They hadn't signed up to the Geneva Convention. They regarded us as slaves. That's what we were and that's how they treated us. Life meant nothing to them. You worked or you died.

The prisoner-of-war camp where Ted Davis was held captive for three and a half years.

They starved us, they worked us to death and they gave us nothing, nothing at all. In the three and a half years that I was a prisoner we received no soap, and no clothing until the end of the war, when they gave us one pair of shorts and a singlet. Rations were one cup of ground rice in the mornings, before you went out to do your labours, a cup of boiled rice and a cup of boiled cabbage and cucumber midday, and the same in the evening. That was it. And if you remained in camp and had no access to any other food, you died, because it wasn't sufficient to keep you alive. Despite the hardships of going out on working parties – and you went out on working parties every day, slaving – you had a chance to pick up some natural food somewhere and that's what kept you alive. That's what I did. I survived because I wouldn't give up. You knew out there that your chances were not very good, but you still did your best to stay alive and to do that you had to get some extra food. It was only food, food. That's what you wanted.

You turned your nose up at nothing. Anything edible, you ate it. You didn't think to yourself, 'I wonder if there's any bacteria on that.' Many things grow wild, like tapioca root which was like a potato and you could come across that.

Australian troops pay tribute to the dead at Kuching prisoner-of-war camp cemetery.

There are snails, there are snakes and we ate those. A snake wasn't bad at all. We used to kill them either by grabbing them by the tail and smacking their heads on the ground, or more often than not by using the tool that we used for digging, which was like a big garden hoe. You would hit it on the head with the garden hoe and that would kill it instantly. The Japanese guards didn't encourage us doing this, but they didn't try and stop us. They thought it was disgusting, but it never occurred to them that it was something we had to do. On one occasion we were cutting down trees to make a landing strip for the Japanese and there was a hollow tree with an armadillo or something like it in there. We took that back to camp, cooked it up for the rest. Otherwise you had no meat at all. On one occasion they brought in a hammerhead shark that had been caught and that was cut up and stewed. But it was survival of the fittest. We used to feel ourselves around the ribs to see how much weight we'd lost, how much flesh we'd lost. You could feel yourself losing weight. You could see it too. Normally I'm around 11½ stone, but I was 6 stone something when we came out.

Many didn't keep going, they just died. It was quite frequent. You'd hear the reveille in the morning from the bugler to wake you up and the chap either next to you or next to someone else didn't wake up: he was dead. But you didn't tell anyone until you'd collected the hut's rations and then you had the full ration with one less to serve. We had no beds and we just slept on the floor, no bed clothing or anything like that. In fact, any clothing we did have either wore out or we found out that we could trade some of it with the local people, perhaps for a bottle of coconut oil or a couple of dried fish or some boiled rice wrapped up in a banana skin, till eventually we had no clothes or shoes at all. So the Japanese issued us with an article of clothing which consisted of a piece of tape with a piece of black cloth attached to it. You tied the tape round your waist and the cloth went up under your crotch and that was your clothing. We used to have to go into Kuching on working parties and they took great delight in marching us dressed like that, no shoes or anything.

Then of course there was the beatings. They beat you any time they felt like it, for no reason. Any infringement and you were beaten up. If you tried to escape, and there was no chance of escaping in a place like Borneo, then they'd just shoot you. The first occasion I got really beaten up was when we were

The guards at Kuching presided over a brutal regime of slave labour.

working at a fuel dump in the centre of Kuching. The chap in charge then was a Japanese sergeant who we named Satan. Our job was stacking fuel drums and loading trucks to carry them away. On this particular day we'd ended the shift and we were pushing the trucks into their shelter, half a dozen of us round each truck, pushing, when for some unknown reason, just because he felt like it, Satan singled me out. I went over to him and I got a severe beating up. Shortly after that beating up I got a bad discharge from my ear, so I went to see Colonel King, who was our medical officer there, and he treated it as best he could, but Satan had perforated my ear. And they would do that sort of thing for no reason at all. They'd hit you with anything they had in their hand.

Other times they would inflict some form of torture on you. They'd make you pick up a heavy lump of stone and hold it above your ahead until they told you to put it down. Or they'd fill a bucket of water and tell you to put that between your knees and stay like that. Another thing they would do if you were out on a working party, they'd line the working party up in two lines facing each other and then they'd force you to knock blazes out of each other, hitting each other around the head. And they'd walk behind and if you weren't doing it good enough for them, they'd wallop you with whatever they had in their hand. But it didn't have any effect because we were just numb.

You didn't really expect to survive. I don't think we would have if they hadn't dropped the atom bomb on Hiroshima. No one would have survived. You couldn't compare it with the German prison camps because you were slaves and they could do with you as they wished. And they did. You couldn't resist because if you resisted, you died. We had a special team of four fellas and they were the burial party; it was their job to dig the graves and bury those that had died. The bodies were just wrapped in a sack and they were put in a coffin, which was made in the camp, and the coffin had a false bottom on it with a latch. When they got to the cemetery, they put the coffin over the hole, the bottom dropped out and the body dropped into the hole.

We used to be roused at six in the morning and then at 8 o'clock we would march out to start work. And at 6 o'clock in the evening, normally, we would pack up and march back to the camp. They had us moving a hill, transferring the soil and the earth from the hill down to the riverside to build it up to make a platform for these ships they were building. Well, we started doing that manually. Those with the hoe would rake the earth into baskets and another chap would put the basket on his head, walk down to the river bank, tip it down and walk back and fill the basket up again. We did that for a week or so, but it wasn't fast enough, so they brought in these steel rails and steel trolleys.

We laid these rails and instead of using the baskets, we filled the trolleys up and we ran down with the trolleys full of earth, then we pushed them back up to fill them again. But on the way down, the Japanese guards would stand by the side of the rails and they'd wallop you as you went past to make you go faster. Later on, things still weren't going fast enough for them, so they introduced a 'speedo' period, where everything the Japanese said to you was 'speedo, speedo, speedo'. And that's when the knocking about and the beatings got worse, because we weren't going fast enough. It was exhausting.

We suffered from lots of diseases. Dysentery was very weakening and you were running to the loo all the time, but there were no proper loos, it was just 5-gallon drums. There was another special party who were employed in emptying these drums every day into the big cesspit that was dug. And I don't want to sound crude but there was no paper either. The only thing that the MO prescribed for dysentery was rice water, the water that the rice was cooked in, because that's thick and starchy, and that did eventually overcome it. Malaria, you just suffered it, no quinine or anything like that. Those people who had a blanket, and I had a half a blanket, would pile them on top of you if you had a rigor. I don't know if you've ever seen anyone with malaria, but when you're having a rigor, you're shaking and you're freezing to death. They'd pile all the blankets on you until the

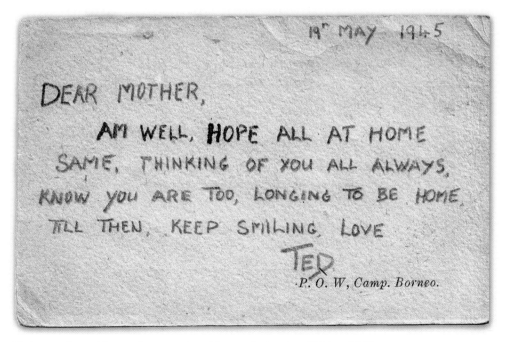

Ted was allowed to send one postcard home, but not until May 1945.

rigor passes. Beriberi was a lack of some vitamin, and your skin puffs up with water. You press it in and it won't come back out again. The only cure for that, as I understand it, is vitamins. Some people got tropical ulcers. If you got a prick on a bit of bamboo or something when you were out on a working party, it would develop into a tropical ulcer. And it would channel itself up inside your leg and come out somewhere else. My pal out there Charlie had terrific tropical ulcers and he couldn't walk hardly, not well enough to go out on a working party.

In the prison camp, you never thought of home. For one thing, throughout the three and half years that I was a prisoner, they never allowed us to receive or send any letters, so you had no news from home at all and they had no news of you. It wasn't until almost the end of the war with Japan, I think it was 25 May 1945, they allowed us to send one postcard, letting our families know we were still alive. We knew the war in Europe was over because one of the chaps had built a radio, but the Japanese didn't broadcast the news throughout the camp. By that time things were getting a little easier because the Japanese had almost given up on us: they knew what was coming. But it was a delicate time because we didn't know what their reaction would be to prisoners.

We found out later what they did to the Australians at Sandakan. There was about 2,300 Australians at Sandakan and a few British Air Force people. That was a dreadful camp and when the end approached for the Japanese, the camp commandant there loaded these Australians with supplies and marched them into the jungle to another base camp about 30 miles inland. They were all starved and on the way many dropped out, and as they dropped out they were shot. In the end, of that 2,300, six survived – that's all, six. That was intended for our camp. Prior to the war ending, we paraded on the square in the camp in front of the Japanese medical officer, Yamamoto his name was. He sat down at a table while we marched in front of him. And he was selecting who would march and who would stay in the camp, and that was going to happen on 15 September, the same thing that happened at Sandakan, but the Australians found out about it and they kept a Beaufighter plane overhead until they could get to us.

When the Japanese did surrender, planes came over and dropped leaflets informing us, so that's how we found out. You had no emotion really. It was survival and I suppose that by then quite a few of the men went past caring whether they survived or not, but I was determined. We were taken off by the American Navy because we were way up river in Sarawak. They sent these PT boats up the river and took us to an American supply ship.

I never returned home until November 1945. When I arrived, I knocked on the door of the house I'd left and my family weren't living there. They'd moved

The general of Kuching camp signs the surrender document.

British soldiers finally leave the camp. In the cockpit of the boat, on the far left, is Medical Officer Colonel King, who treated Ted Davis's perforated ear.

next door because our old home had been damaged during an air raid. My sister greeted me at the door; I had three sisters and one brother. Then I met my mother and father, and it wasn't an enthusiastic greeting. I mean I was a stranger really. There was a kiss, but there was no embrace really. And then I said to my mother, 'Where's my brother?' He was in the Somerset Light Infantry and he'd been mobilised in September 1939. They told me that he'd died on the Normandy beaches, so I didn't know that until I got home.

I'd thought about remaining in the Army, I liked the Army, but I thought my mother went through the drama of first me being missing and then a prisoner of war and then getting another telegram saying my brother was killed, so I couldn't leave home. I used to go out for a couple of drinks, perhaps one too

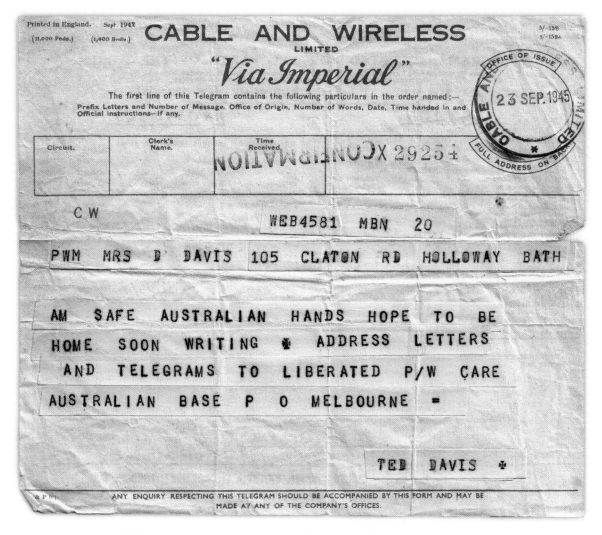

Ted Davis felt like a stranger when he returned home to Bath.

many, because I felt sad and lonely and I missed the camaraderie of the Army. My girlfriend wasn't there when I came home either, but that turned out for the best. One day I was out with an old school pal and we went to a dance in Bath. During the 'ladies' excuse me' a lady came up to me and asked me for a dance. We courted and we've been married ever since.

Bibliography

'4th/1st Gurkhas at Kohima 1944, The', *The Bugle and Kukri*, 2000

Ambrose, S.E, *Pegasus Bridge*, Pocket Books, 1985

Clark, L., *Orne Bridgehead*, Sutton Publishing, 2004

Conyers Nesbit, R., *The Battle of the Atlantic*, Sutton Publishing, 2002

Fane, J., *A Diary of the Days Spent in Action in Belgium and France, 1940*, Private Collection

Ford, K., *Sword Beach*, Sutton Publishing, 2004

Gilmore, E.M.B, 'Cassel, May 1940', *Back Badge*, 1946

Henn, F.R., 'A Narrow Escape', *Back Badge*, winter 1992

Humphries, S., *The Call of the Sea, Britain's Maritime Past 1900–1960*, BBC Books, 1997

Jackson, R., *Dunkirk, The British Evacuation 1940*, Cassell Military Paperbacks, 1976

Lake, J., *The Battle of Britain*, Silverdale Books, 2000

Never Feared a Foe of Any Kind, A Short History of the Gloucestershire Regiment 1694 – 1991

Priestley, F.W., 'The 5th Glosters at Ledringhem', *Back Badge*, 1946

Shephard, M., 'Grindorff', *Back Badge*, 1950

Thompson, J., *The Imperial War Museum Book of the War in Burma, 1942–1945*, Sidgwick & Jackson, 2002

Warner, P., *The Battle of France, 1940*, Cassell Military Paperbacks, 1990

Watkins, D., *Fear Nothing, The History of No.501 (County of Gloucester) Fighter Squadron*, Newton Publishers, 1990

Williams, A., *The Battle of the Atlantic*, BBC Worldwide Ltd, 2002

Wilson, P., *Dunkirk, From Disaster to Deliverance*, Leo Cooper, 1999

Wyvern in North West Europe, The: Being a Short History of the 43rd Wessex Division 24 June 1944–8 May 1945

Young, G., *Private Young's War*, The Royal Gloucestershire, Berkshire and Wiltshire Regiment Wardrobe and Museum Trust, 2004

Index